FOX
The Complete Guide to
Carp Fishing

THE COMPLETE GUIDE TO CARP FISHING

First Published in 2008 by Fox International Group Ltd,
Fowler Road, Hainault Business Park, Hainault, Essex. IG6 3UT.
United Kingdom
TEL:- +44 (0) 208 559 6500
FAX:- +44 (0) 208 501 1655
E Mail:- info@foxint.com
Web:- www.foxint.com

Designed and produced by the Creative Team at Fox International.

Written by Colin Davidson. Photography by Colin Davidson, Roy
Westwood and Greg Meenehan. Additional photography by the Fox
consultants.

CONTENTS

Chapter 1   LOCATION AND BEHAVIOUR   *008 - 035*

Chapter 2   CARP CARE   *036 - 045*

Chapter 3   END TACKLES   *046 - 065*

Chapter 4   LINES   *066 - 077*

Chapter 5   SPODDING   *078 - 089*

Chapter 6   ACCURACY AND FEEDING   *090 - 103*

Chapter 7   THE METHOD   *104 - 115*

Chapter 8   STALKING   *116 - 123*

Chapter 9   SNAG FISHING   *124 - 135*

Chapter 10   FLOATER FISHING   *136 - 153*

Chapter 11   WINTER FISHING   *154 - 169*

Chapter 12   RIG PRINCIPLES   *170 - 187*

Chapter 13   ADVANCED RIGS   *188 -205*

Chapter 14   BOILIES   *206 - 213*

Chapter 15   PARTICLE BAITS   *214 - 221*

Chapter 16   PELLETS   *222 - 227*

Chapter 17   PVA   *228 - 243*

I am wonderfully fortunate to be surrounded by words and pictures concerning carp fishing every day of my working life and have been privy to many books, guides and other literature, some more impressive than others.

Back in 2005 I wrote the foreword to the Fox Guide to Modern Carp Fishing which stood out as being a cut above many of the other instructional books available at the time. In this new offering the Complete Guide to Carp Fishing Fox have produced a book which yet again sets the standard - perhaps for a long time to come.

There is something in this book for everyone, whether you are looking for your first double or 20-pounder or are a seasoned carper with numbers of big fish under your belt looking to glean some of the secrets for success that the Fox consultants rely on to keep them at the top of the sport.

From the very basics such as understanding your quarry and how carp behave through to tying cutting-edge presentations, the very latest in computer aided graphics, expert photography and diagrams help take you step by step from start to finish.

With the expertise of anglers such as Colin Davidson, Ian Chillcott, Chris Rose and Steve Spurgeon you cannot fail to improve as a carp angler. Such a wealth of information comes from more years of hard experience behind the rods catching carp year in year out than these guys would probably like us to add up.

Packed with common sense advice covering everything from carp care to spodding, feature finding, PVA, bait choice and rig principles I think those of us with a few more years under our belt can only look at this book and wish we had had something similar available many years ago to prevent us making so many simple mistakes and learning the hard way!

The Fox brand is synonymous with quality and the quality and class we have become accustomed to in Fox products shines through in this book. It's the most comprehensive instructional volume I've yet seen in a long time and can't fail to help you catch more and bigger carp.

Marc Coulson.

TotalCarp

Marc is the editor of Total Carp, the UK's biggest selling monthly carp title – on sale the last Friday of every month.

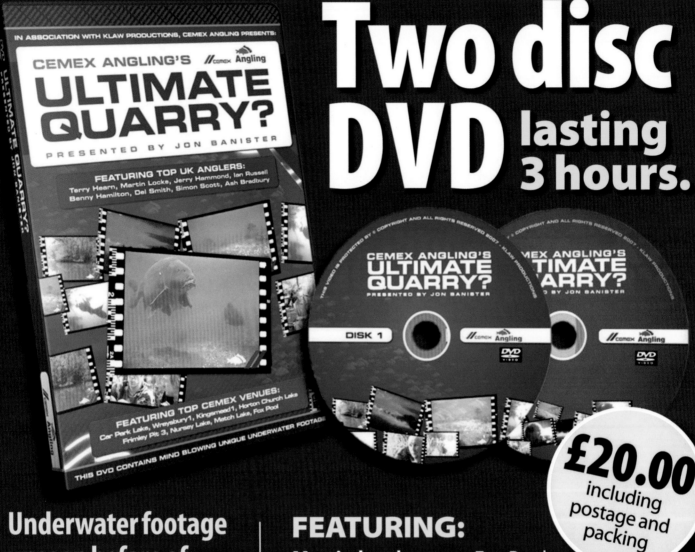

CHAPTER 1
LOCATION AND
CARP BEHAVIOUR

SUPERSENSE CARP

HOW much do you know about the fish you are trying to catch? Carp are fascinating creatures, with such broad appeal that they are by far the most popular sport species in the UK, and possibly across Europe.

Individual in scaling, shape and even character, hard fighting and showing an incredible ability to learn far beyond that of other species the carp is a challenging quarry. Unlike just 50 years ago when their behaviour was still shrouded in mystery and carp were the elusive monsters of freshwater, we now have a wider appreciation of their life cycle, habits and more importantly how to catch them.

It's a testament to the effectiveness of modern tactics and baits that even raw beginners with minimal angling background have the chance to catch plenty of carp, but an interest in and understanding of their life cycle, senses and behaviour can only help give a greater appreciation of how to catch them. What do they smell or taste? What do they see when we're looking at fish basking under our noses. What is it that alarms them or puts them on their guard?

Hundreds of thousands of years of evolution has equipped carp to survive in their underwater environment, us trying to catch them is just another possible source of danger for their senses to alert them to.

"What do carp smell or taste? What do they see when we're looking at fish basking under our noses?"

EYESIGHT

Carp have tremendous eyesight, and one of the biggest recent advances in understanding carp behaviour is the wide appreciation of how keenly carp see lines, end tackles and even the smallest rig bits. It's no coincidence that camouflage, drab, non-reflective finishes and carefully chosen colours are evident throughout the Fox range of terminal tackle.

Carp eyes are evolved to work in water and in much lower light levels than the human eye. Because of their position on the head carp have a limited field of binocular (two eye) vision, and have blind spots very close in front of the nose and behind the tail, but can see along their flanks.

Anyone who keeps koi or carp in a pond will also know that in strong light carp readily see out of water. Appearing out the back door can be enough to excite carp in a pond at the bottom of a garden into thinking they might be fed even if they are 20 or 30 yards away. Movement rather than shape is the big giveaway, in a more natural situation fast or unexpected movements always put carp on their guard. However, when a carp is removed from water its eyes stop functioning so well, vision limited to just a few centimetres.

It's thought carp have extensive colour vision, possibly extending beyond the range we see, and anecdotal evidence also suggests that a carp's eyes are sensitive to light outside the visible light spectrum, for example the infra-red beams of camera flashguns.

In bright sunshine and clear water anything you can see underwater you can expect a carp to see clearly too - and probably more besides.

If you snip the points off even drab Teflon coated hooks and leave them in an aquarium carp will very quickly home in on them and pick them up to see what they are.

Sight is not vital for feeding, and in murky waters or when silt feeding taste and smell are the key senses.

It's not unusual for carp to suffer blindness from damage or disease and still survive quite happily, but never underestimate the clarity and perception a carp has through its eyes. Although the senses of taste and smell are much more important for finding food carp see everything we see and plenty more - remember this when approaching a carp session.

"Anything you can see underwater you can expect a carp to see too - and more besides"

EVER sniffed a bait and thought it wasn't very strongly flavoured? It's unlikely a carp would do the same - they have a hugely developed sense of smell that allows them to detect some chemicals at levels as low as one part in a trillion. That's the equivalent of one teaspoon in 2,000 public swimming pools - how's that for a keen nose?

The nostrils on top of the head are pits that contain the olfactory rosette - a collection of highly folded layers of skin that smell the water passing over them continuously.

Taste in carp comes from taste buds, found in the mouth, and also on the lips, gill rakers in the back of the throat and in low numbers on the fins. These taste buds are activated by contact with food.

Carp often suck in all manner of sediment and detect whether food is present through contact with the palantine organ, a sensitive area in the roof of the mouth which also constantly tastes inhaled water as they swim around.

Whether carp detect the same basic types of taste as humans is difficult to gauge but they respond positively to all manner of foods including sweet, savoury and even very spicy.

HEARING

You can't see them but carp do have ears. Because a carp is mostly made up of water itself it is effectively transparent to sound in water, needing a higher density structure to detect vibrations passing through the water around it.

Ear bones called otoliths and the swimbladder perform this function. The otoliths are inside the head just behind the skull in fluid filled chambers lined with hair cells that pick up vibrations. The swimbladder changes in volume slightly as vibrations hit it, these are transmitted via small bones to the inner ear, giving very good hearing.

The lateral line also helps detect vibration from other fish. A fluid filled canal along the flanks of the fish also containing sensory 'hairs' it detects water movement through vibration along the canal - helping it detect the source of vibration as the nearest flank receives the strongest signal.

Carp hear low frequency sounds best, meaning they can't probably hear a high tone bite alarm, but a heavy footfall on the bank will give you away long before you even get your bite alarms out.

* Information courtesy of The Sparsholt Guide to the Management of Carp Fisheries (2001) Edited by Chris Seagrave. ISBN: 0-9540054-0-6

LOCATION AND FEATURE FINDING USING YOUR EYES

FOR MANY feature finding means marker float work and plumbing depths, but good location skills begin long before a marker rod is even taken out of your holdall.

It can be a great help being able to identify bars, shallows, deeps, humps and bumps in different swims, and all can be productive areas to position hook baits, but your eyes are your most important location tool of all no matter what type of venue you are tackling.

All the Fox Carp Team would agree that several hours spent walking around a venue and watching for signs of carp can be a bigger help to correct swim choice than several hours spent casting and retrieving a marker float.

Any experienced angler will have caught lots of carp from swims or lakes that they know very little about in terms of charting depths or underwater features. Gathering information through observation and through spending time fishing is more than enough to help you catch carp on plenty of modern venues, no matter how pressurised.

"Your eyes are your most important location tool no matter what type of venue you are fishing"

POLARISING GLASSES

ARGUABLY the most vital piece of modern carp angling kit and yet still not carried by thousands of carpers, polarising glasses open up another dimension of understanding of the underwater world.

Polarising lenses cut down reflection and glare from the surface of water, resulting in vastly improved underwater vision. Wearing glasses can allow you to clearly see fish feeding, travelling sub-surface or sitting in the upper layers.
Not wearing polarising glasses often leaves you unable to see anything. The money spent on good polarising glasses will repay you many times over, and is a far wiser investment for the dedicated carp angler than more bait or new rods.

Lenses in polarising glasses come in different colours, suiting both individual eyesight and specific light conditions, whether in a particular swim or at a certain time of day.

Typically Amber lenses are the best choice in low light levels early and late in the day, allowing you to see where darker lenses cut out too much light. Darker brown lenses provide better definition in very bright conditions, grey lenses are great all-rounders.

The Series 700 glasses recognise the advantages of different colour lenses on different days and are supplied with easily interchangeable cristec polyamid lenses, 99.7% efficient and three times tougher than glass or acrylic. Good glasses are not just invaluable for fishing, they also protect your eyes.

Such high specification lenses in the 700 Series exceed all global standards, protecting against ultra violet light, UVA, UVB and UV400 light rays.

With years of experience manufacturing polarising glasses Fox glasses are accepted as the very best, ergonomically designed for tremendous comfort with unrivalled performance, value for money and style.

WITHOUT POLARISING LENSES

WITH POLARISING LENSES

PRIMARY LOCATION CLUES

. Finding numbers of carp crashing or head and shouldering should establish choice of swim without any feature finding required.

3. In strong sunlight bars or plateaux can often be seen through polarising glasses, typically showing up yellow.

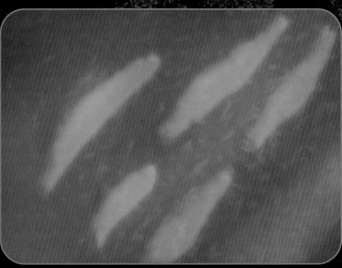

2. Cruising carp can often be seen with the naked eye, wearing polarising glasses shows them more clearly and even when the water is rippled.

4. Getting a higher perspective and looking down, either from up a tree or from any man made vantage point allows you to see deeper into the water.

5. Bubbling or coloured, muddied water are great giveaways that carp are feeding or have recently been feeding in an area of a lake.

. Wind direction often dictates where carp want to be. Check the windward margin for signs of fish activity, especially on a fresh wind or a very big blow.

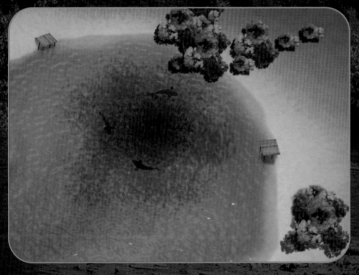

. Always check for signs of carp in the margins. On pits look for clean, yellow gravel margins particularly around cover such as overhanging trees. Carp can often be spotted patrolling or laying up.

. Are other anglers catching or blanking? On busier and larger waters where the action is happening can help you narrow down swim choices.

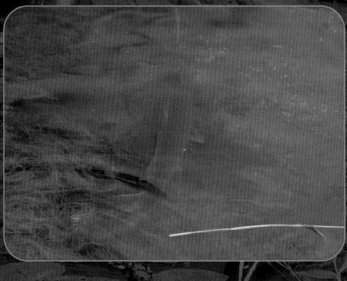

FEELING YOUR LEAD DOWN

A KEY skill in fishing effectively and confidently without using a marker float is feeling your lead down after it hits the water until it touches down on the lake bed, helping you determine the depth of a swim and the nature of the bottom you are fishing over.

1. Use an end tackle with a 2-4 oz lead. Feeling leads down is easiest when conditions are calm. Don't attempt to practice or master the technique when there are huge gusting winds that belly your line on the cast.

2. With experience you can also register different lake beds when casting PVA bags and Method feeder rigs but because they sink more slowly and touch down more lightly it is more difficult to interpret. Stick to end tackles just with leads initially.

3. Towards the end of the cast feather the line using your forefinger to slow the rate the line leaves the spool and straighten the line from rod tip to rig. As the rig hits the surface trap the line on the spool with your finger.

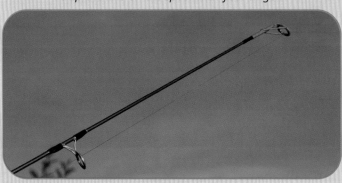

5. When the rig touches bottom the rod tip will spring back and some slack line is created at the rod tip. The type of sensation you feel through the rod and on your finger tip at the reel when the rig touches bottom tells you what you have landed over.

4. Keeping the rod tip high and your finger on the reel spool you will feel the line tighten from rod tip to lead as it sinks. The rod tip is pulled gently towards the water where the rig has landed.

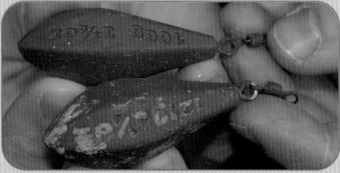

6. It takes practice to interpret the different sensations. Hard rod tip knocks and bangs from gravel, sand and clay are easiest to interpret. Check your end tackle when you retrieve, damaged or marked leads have landed over gravel, clay or chalk.

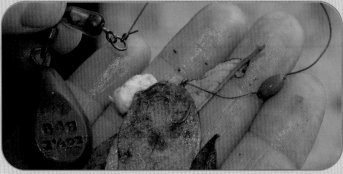

7. If you are bringing back weed, debris or leaf litter and your lead smells you are over thick silt or weed and presentation will be less effective. In water of 3ft or less it is almost impossible to feel a rig down because the lead touches down almost instantly after hitting the surface.

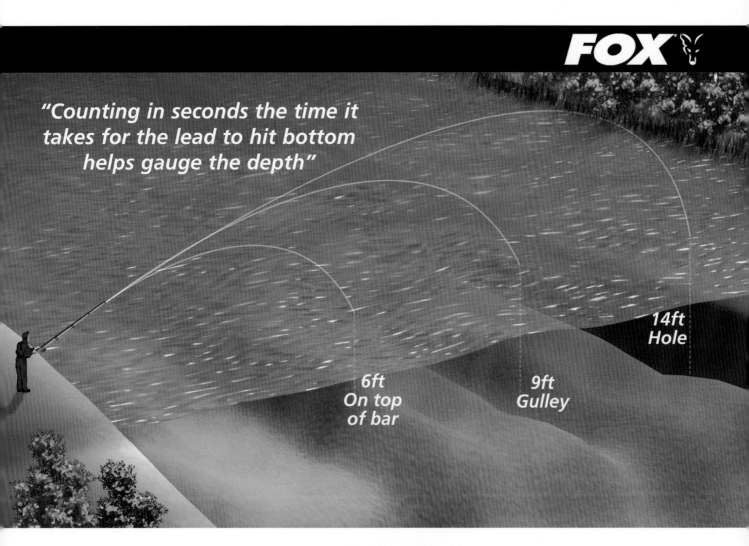

"Counting in seconds the time it takes for the lead to hit bottom helps gauge the depth"

14ft
Hole

6ft
On top
of bar

9ft
Gulley

GAUGING THE DEPTH

FEELING leads down can also be used to give an indication of depths around a swim without using a marker float. Counting in seconds from when the rig hits surface to touching down on the lake bed gives a rough estimate of the depth in feet. As long as you use leads of the same size so their sink rate remains the same you can compare different depths in different areas of a swim to give clues to the location of major features such as bars and plateaux.

SENSATION AT ROD TIP	
FEELING	**LAKE BED**
HARD, SHARP BANG	GRAVEL
ROUNDED, CLEAN THUD	SAND OR CLAY
NO DISTINCT MOVEMENT	WEED
SOFT RELEASE OF PRESSURE	SILT

SETTING UP A MARKER FLOAT RIG

TO SAVE tackling and retackling, a marker rod left made up between sessions is invaluable. Purpose designed marker rods cast heavy leads and large markers yet remain responsive in the tip to interpret the lake bed your lead is being retrieved across. Depth measures at the butt allow you to accurately chart changes in depth and pinpoint hotspots. Fox marker rods have measures at six and 12 inches to help locate even the smallest variations that can easily be missed.

Twinning a marker rod with a free spool reel makes it quicker and easier to feed line from the reel to pop marker floats to the surface than repeatedly slackening clutches. Marker reels should be spooled up with Dyneema braid. The low diameter and lack of stretch of braided reel lines like Fox Submerge allows markers to be cast long distances and the lake bed to be interpreted more accurately.

HOW TO SET-UP A MARKER FLOAT

1. For all but extreme range work a mono leader helps a marker float pop up more easily. Join the first two rod lengths (lowest diameter) of a Fox tapered mono leader to the braid on the reel with a double grinner.

2. Fox marker float kits contain everything you need for an effective marker set-up in one blister pack. Micro Markers are great all-rounders, ideal for ranges up to 60-70 yards.

3. Thread the tapered mono leader through the rings. Thread on the Slik Ring and clip on one of the Speed Links. The Slik ring features a Zirconia insert to minimise friction and ensure marker floats pop up readily.

4. Follow the Slik ring with the high diameter rubber stop bead, tie the remaining Speed Link on the end of the leader then push the rubber bead down over the knot.

5. A standard Explorer Lead and one attached to a metal link are supplied in marker kits. The lead on the link helps keep the Slik ring above the lake bed to reduce the chance of it being jammed by weed, silkweed, leaf litter or debris from thick silt.

6. Attach a marker of your choice to the Speed Link on the end of the leader depending upon the venue, the range being fished and the light conditions in front of your swim.

WHICH FLOAT?

DIFFERENT situations demand different floats. It helps to match the float and lead to the situation. On smaller waters or for closer spots a Micro Marker with a 2 oz Explorer lead causes much less disturbance. For longer range the Horizon Marker with a 3 or 4 oz lead is designed to fly long distances and remain visible at ranges well over 100 yards. The Weed Marker has a bulbous body to increase buoyancy and allow it to surface even when weed stems impede less buoyant designs.

"Pinpointing small hotspots can bring big rewards"

VISIBLE AND VERSATILE

SPENDING time pinpointing productive underwater features, then being unable to fish them effectively because a marker float is difficult to see is a fruitless exercise. Light conditions change in a swim as a result of different weather or even at different times of day but casting and feeding need to be accurate at all times. Fox Horizon and Weed Markers are both supplied with interchangeable sight tips, allowing them to be unscrewed and changed in seconds to maintain maximum visibility and accuracy. The Micro Marker Kit contains three colour variant floats. Fluoro orange is the best all-round choice, black sight tips the best option in choppy white water conditions on larger more exposed venues and fluoro yellow excelling against dark water backdrops such as against overhangs and shaded far margins.

"Interchangeable sight tips maintain visibility and accuracy"

LOCATING FEATURES

PLUMBING a swim and dragging a lead back across the lake bed is the best way we have of locating key underwater features. It requires care, attention to detail and accurate recording of what you find to make the biggest differences to your catch rate. There's little point in locating attractive subsurface features only not to be able to find them a second time or on subsequent sessions. Here's how to map out swims quickly and efficiently.

1. It's easiest to map a swim out methodically from one side to the other. Steadily plumb and feel the bottom further left or right with each cast until you have covered all of the available water.

2. After the marker has landed sweep the rod tip back so the float is drawn back tight to the lead. Keeping the rod steady peel a foot of line from the free spool, and count the line pulled off the reel until the float pops up. Marker rods have depth markers on the butt so you peel exactly a foot of line every time for accuracy.

3. After recording the depth, pull the float back down until you feel it locked up at the lead. Gently pull the lead towards you one metre at a time keeping the rod low to maintain contact with the lake bed. Now feed the float up and check the depth again.

4. Write the depths you record down in a notebook or diary so you can refer to it when you are fishing to find features quicker, or without using a marker at all.

5. Once you've found an interesting or substantial feature always record the direction it is found in using skyline or sight markers as a reference. These can be taller trees, distinctive shapes or changes in the top of the tree line, pylons, telegraph poles or even buildings.

6. If the direction of a feature doesn't easily cross reference with an obvious skyline or sight marker walk up or down the bank to the left or right and see if it lines up more easily when casting from somewhere else. There's no rule that you must stand in the centre of a swim.

TOP TIP - Keep recording depths until the lead and float are right under your feet. You can often find some lovely features that produce lots of carp very close in that others don't find because they are more interested in feature finding further out.

FISHING BY FEEL

Recording the nature of the lake bed is as important as charting depths. As you pull the lead and float back the zero stretch on the braided line will help reveal what the bottom is like. In the same way it takes practice to recognise the different sensations on a rod tip when you feel a lead down to the bottom, interpreting the lake bed from dragging a lead also takes practice.

SENSATION ON ROD TIP	LAKE BED
SHARP TAPS, BANGS AND RATTLES	GRAVEL
LEAD MOVES EASILY AND SMOOTHLY AS IF ACROSS GLASS	SAND OR CLAY
LOCKS UP, THEN FREES FROM STEADY PRESSURE. FEELS LIKE PULLING A DEAD WEIGHT TOWARDS YOU.	WEED
LOCKS UP INITIALLY THEN SLOWLY PULLS FREE. LEAD FEELS AS IF MOVEMENTS ARE DAMPENED/HEAVY	SILT

LEAD LIFTING

FEELING the lake bed is much less accurate if the lead is lifted off bottom as the marker float rig is dragged back towards the angler. Light leads with highly buoyant floats will cause leads to lift off bottom, reducing sensitivity. Explorer Leads are a weight forward design with CAD designed probes to maximise transmission of vibration back through the line to the rod and reel but rely on continued contact with the bottom for optimum performance. Use 2-3 oz leads with Micro Markers and 3-4 oz leads with Horizon and Weed Markers for optimum performance. Keeping the rod parallel to the water and drawing the lead and marker slowly back to you is more effective than holding the rod upright which lifts the lead off bottom.

MARKER FLOAT WORK

THERE is a time and place to investigate swims using marker floats, but it pays to remember it isn't always an essential ingredient for catching carp. Marker floats help us understand where and how hook baits might be best placed on some venues to give us an increased chance of success.

But it can take several hours and many, many casts to build up even a basic mental picture of a swim and the disturbance caused can be enough to spook any carp that were present in the swim when you arrived. Whether to use a marker float is a decision based on common sense and experience,

but it pays to remember that a less well presented hook bait put in front of feeding fish in a swim you are fishing blind will always catch more than a hook bait presented with pinpoint accuracy on an underwater feature if you've spooked all the carp out the swim trying to find that spot in the first place.

"Using a marker float isn't always an essential ingredient for catching carp"

WHEN TO PLUMB

1. During the winter or Close Season (with permission) to map out key swims and features. Recording depths, directions, distances and sight lines allows you to present baits on key features with minimal disturbance when fishing.

2. On very busy venues where there is regular disturbance from leads, spods and baiting up around you there is little advantage in not feature finding to locate potential hotspots.

3. At the end of a session you can plumb a swim or two to help build pictures of different parts of a lake without disturbing your swim when fishing.

4. When thick weed or silt makes good presentation of hook baits difficult in much of a swim, use a marker rod to find clear areas or areas of harder bottom.

5. For longer sessions of several days it can help to map out a swim in the beginning to ensure efficient placement of feed and hook baits for the rest of the session.

6. Some gravel pits are tremendously complex in their underwater topography. Plumbing pits is much more helpful than plumbing reservoirs, commercial fisheries or estate lakes.

WHEN NOT TO PLUMB

1. When there is lots of carp activity in front of you like crashing, head and shouldering or rolling. Repeated casting will spook fish away, cast hook baits instead for the first few hours.

2. When a venue is quiet or you are well away from the disturbance of other anglers using a marker float will disturb carp that have found refuge in a quieter area of a lake.

3. Estate lakes, meres, reservoirs, commercial venues, rivers and canals rarely have substantial underwater features. Observation and the feel of a lead hitting the bottom is as useful as a marker float.

4. Plumbing during short sessions reduces your chances of catching. Carp will often return to areas they want to be in even if they are alarmed by casting, but if time is short it might not be until long after you pack up.

5. When margin fishing or at very short range marker floats are unnecessary. Depth of water and nature of the bottom can be judged by feeling leads down on the cast, or even lowering them off the rod tip in very close spots.

6. If arriving at dawn or when a fishery first opens watch for signs of carp rather than plumbing. You can often catch carp quickly by casting at signs of fish. Plumbing can wait until later in the day when feeding activity slows or stops.

LOCATING CARP ON GRAVEL PITS

INACCESSIBLE AREAS
Many mature pits have substantial woodland surrounding them, preventing swims being evenly distributed. Take stalking gear and check out areas where there are no swims to catch even difficult carp off guard.

WINDWARD BANKS
From April to October carp are often found on the windward bank in coloured water looking for food. Carp react fast to changing weather, moving long distances in minutes.

SNAGS
Anywhere carp can find safety will draw and hold fish, from sunken blocks of concrete and rubble, to discarded machinery and metalwork or more orthodox fallen trees and roots.

OUT OF RANGE AREAS
Regularly shaped pits don't have to be large for areas to be difficult to reach, where carp will crash and show repeatedly. If you can cast further than other anglers such areas can be incredibly productive.

WEEDBEDS
Offering oxygenation, shelter and natural food carp will spend weeks or months frequenting large weedbeds. Through the winter weedbeds retain heat. Excellent for spring sport when fresh plant growth emerges.

SILT TROUGHS
A build up of sediment by wind and undertow creates silt deposits behind and between bars, often rich in natural foods like bloodworm and tubifex.

BAR INTERSECTIONS AND GAPS
Anywhere that bars intersect funnels carp through small areas, making great ambush points.

BARS

Common to all wet dug pits, bars are long ridges formed by the massive scoops that extract gravel. Often they lie parallel, pits typically worked from one end to the other. Key travel routes, navigation points and feeding areas.

SHALLOWS

Anywhere the sun warms water quickly you will find carp. Shallower bays or margins are rich in natural food. Depending on when they receive the sun carp visit at different times of the day.

POINTS

Often the remains of roadways where gravel was extracted in trucks. Points and spits often continue as large bars and offer lots of water and good visibility.

SUNKEN ROADWAYS

In dry dug pits major bars were roadways for machinery in and out as it was worked. Huge navigation and feeding features.

BAYS

Bays on any venue can be stuffed with carp or devoid. Check them out if they are on the end of a fresh wind or receive lots of sunshine early and late season. Also often productive on floaters in the summer.

MARGINS

No matter how big the venue, still the number one feature. Look for clean sloping gravel shelves, lilies, overhanging trees and bushes.

LOCATING CARP ON ESTATE LAKES

SHALLOWS
Commonly silting up towards a feeder stream, estate lakes often feature shallows with extensive reedbeds, tree cover or inaccessible areas that are havens for carp.

FEEDER STREAM
A source of oxygenated water and food, an inlet is always attractive to carp, especially through the warmer months.

NATURAL FOOD LARDERS
Predominantly silty, estate lakes are full of natural food like bloodworm and tubifex. Watch for carp consistently bubbling or fizzing to locate rich feeding areas that will produce takes.

HARD AREAS

Even the siltiest venue will contain areas where carp have scoured the silt clean repeatedly digging around for food. Anywhere that feels harder when a lead or marker float rig lands is a good area for a take.

MONK

Small concrete structures containing wooden boards that are added or removed to govern water flow out of an estate lake or stream fed lake, the monk can be a hotspot for natural food. Monks are often productive in the winter.

DAM WALL

The dam area and deeper water of any estate lake often produces fewer fish but surprisingly often the biggest fish.

MARGINAL LILIES

A feature of many estate lakes, marginal lilies offer sanctuary and feeding opportunities. Stealth is essential when fishing this close.

LOCATING CARP ON COMMERCIAL FISHERIES

MARGINS

The biggest and best feature on most commercial fisheries and the best place to bump into the biggest carp. Match anglers refer to big carp around the margins as kerb crawlers! Stick to a sprinkling of bait and fish for one carp at a time.

OUT OF BOUNDS AREAS

Some commercials have no fishing areas to give sanctuary, the entrance being an obvious area to put hook baits in front of fish, but often very pressurised.

OUT OF BOUNDS

UNDERCUT BANKS

Anywhere there is overhanging foliage or brambles you can find undercuts where carp have dug and hollowed out underneath the bank, often sitting out of harm's way. Look for any marginal plant growth and present baits alongside.

CLOUDED WATER
Where stock levels are high on commercially managed venues any number of carp feeding will create muddied water. Check clarity in the margins along different banks and in corners or bays and watch for muddy slicks appearing.

ISLAND MARGINS
There will always be carp hugging islands on commercial fisheries, but they are the most obvious feature of all so hook baits need to be presented within inches of the margin for the best chance of action.

LESS POPULAR SWIMS/AREAS
Most fisheries have areas that are less well fished, normally the furthest from the car park or the least comfortable. Even if you are restricted to one or two rods instead of three tuck yourself into tight swims as carp always frequent areas away from anglers.

PLATFORMS/SWIMS
Where there are any platforms or staging carp will be quick to nose around underneath them, especially as leftover bait is often chucked in front of them by pleasure anglers. Carp will be so close they are often underneath where you would sit on a platform.

CHAPTER 2

CARP CARE AND GOOD PRACTICE

CARP CARE AND GOOD PRACTICE

1. CARP can easily be damaged before reaching the mat. Before lifting a net always loosen your line from rod tip to net by engaging the free spool on a reel or opening the bale arm and feeding some slack out.

2. If the rod tip is bent round into a net as a carp is moved its fins and body can easily be damaged by end tackle which is often wrapped around the fish as it lies in the bottom of the net.

3. Always check that a carp's fins are flush to its body before carrying whether in a net, sling or sack. A fin that is folded backwards out from the body can easily be snapped or damaged.

4. Nets are easily broken if used incorrectly. If lifting a carp in the net, always support the net cord with one hand and the spreader block with the other. Lifting from the handle only will simply smash the net pole or arms.

5. Carrying a 12 foot rod and six foot net pole can be troublesome in many swims. It's often easiest to release the net arms and mesh from the pole. The Fox carbon folding net has a fast release trigger-lok to allow the arms to be removed and collapsed in seconds.

6. Once the arms have been disengaged from a spreader block carefully roll the arms down together to shorten the mesh. Check fins are flat, line isn't tangled around the carp then carry the net and rod and reel up to the mat.

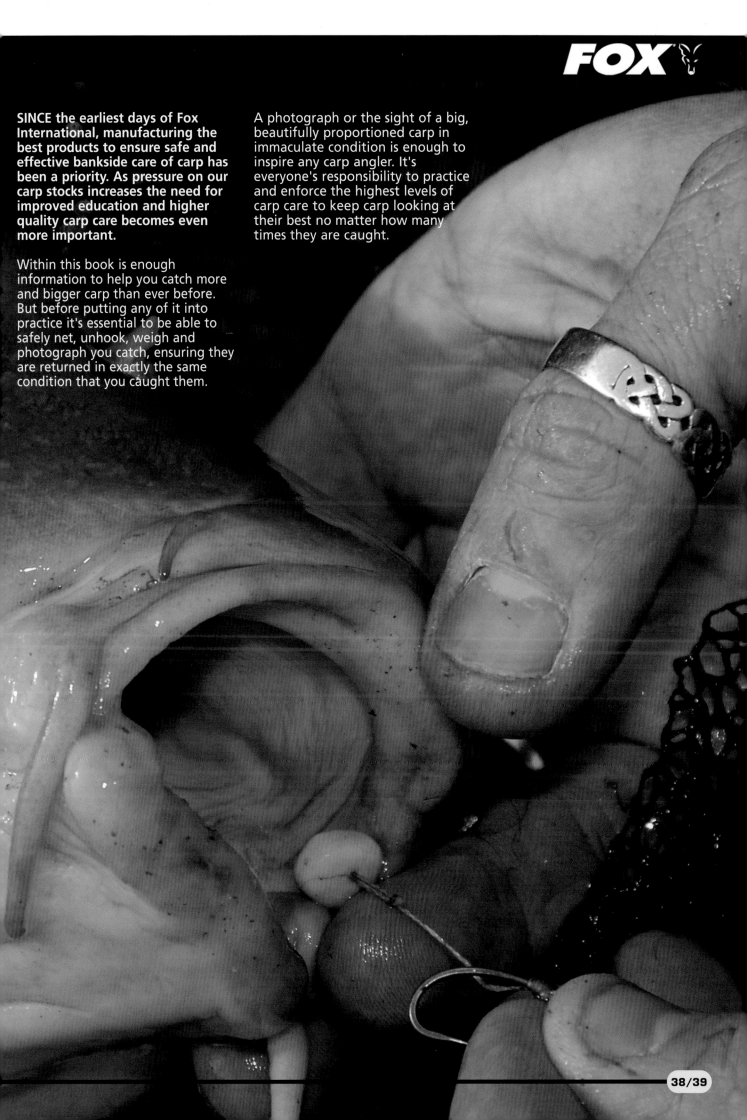

SINCE the earliest days of Fox International, manufacturing the best products to ensure safe and effective bankside care of carp has been a priority. As pressure on our carp stocks increases the need for improved education and higher quality carp care becomes even more important.

Within this book is enough information to help you catch more and bigger carp than ever before. But before putting any of it into practice it's essential to be able to safely net, unhook, weigh and photograph you catch, ensuring they are returned in exactly the same condition that you caught them.

A photograph or the sight of a big, beautifully proportioned carp in immaculate condition is enough to inspire any carp angler. It's everyone's responsibility to practice and enforce the highest levels of carp care to keep carp looking at their best no matter how many times they are caught.

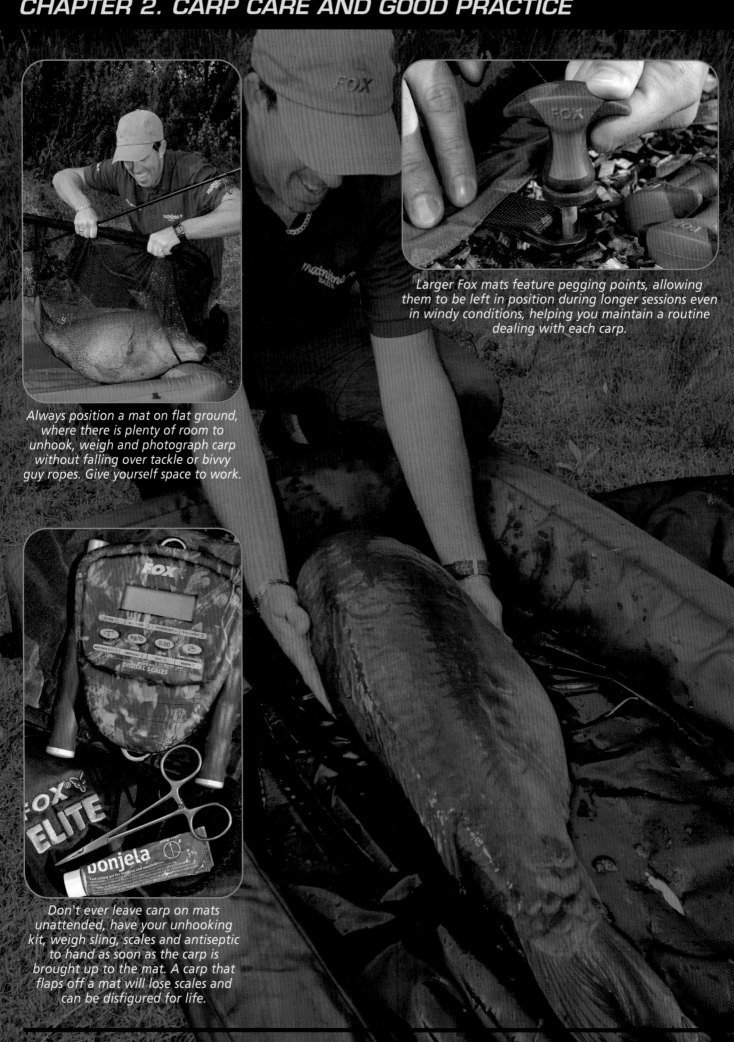

Larger Fox mats feature pegging points, allowing them to be left in position during longer sessions even in windy conditions, helping you maintain a routine dealing with each carp.

Always position a mat on flat ground, where there is plenty of room to unhook, weigh and photograph carp without falling over tackle or bivvy guy ropes. Give yourself space to work.

Don't ever leave carp on mats unattended, have your unhooking kit, weigh sling, scales and antiseptic to hand as soon as the carp is brought up to the mat. A carp that flaps off a mat will lose scales and can be disfigured for life.

WHICH UNHOOKING MAT?

COMPULSORY on almost every carp water, there is no excuse for inadequate unhooking protection, whether fishing for carp, pike, barbel or any other specimen fish.

SO WHICH MAT SHOULD YOU BUY?

Always choose the biggest and most generously padded mat you can afford. Budget is not an excuse for poor carp care. The Fox Stalker Safety Zone mat offers twin protection from a polystrene bean filled outer rim and thick protective foam centre, and is capable of handling carp to 40 lb and beyond comfortably yet costs around £20.00. For less than the cost of two kilos of quality boilies you can buy a mat that will last several seasons and be suitable for carp both in the UK and abroad.

Fox's Safety Zone Carp Cradles are inflatable mat designs that combine the very best padding and protection for carp on the mat thanks to their expanding air cell technology, yet remain protected from puncture on the toughest banks thanks to a tough PVC base and reinforced polyester body. Standard and Euro versions are available.

When inflated the cradles boast a raised outer edge and secure central recess to retain carp. A retaining flap prevents carp jumping out, doubling as a kneeling mat for photography.

Carp are also easily moved safely in the cradle back to the water using tough carry handles. At the end of a session Boston valves deflate the cradles to the size of a weigh sling removing the bulk of a large mat from your kit without sacrificing carp care.

Mats can get very hot when left out in the sun for long periods. Always wet a mat before a carp is placed on it. A bucket or a collapsible Method bowl of lake water next to the mat makes it easy.

Mats offer extra storage options. When folded, mats like the Stalker or the bean filled Elite mat can also be used to carry low chairs, additional clothing and weigh slings. For short sessions and stalking a mat can carry all the tackle you need.

UNHOOKING

MOST modern carp rigs hook fish in the bottom lip or the scissors either side of the mouth. With the sizes of carp hooks in common use unhooking is often easiest with finger and thumb. If possible get hold of the shank or bend of the hook and use firm pressure to push it back out in the direction it came. If the hook is really buried positioning a finger inside a carp's mouth and pushing from the eye using a thumb will usually pop a hook back out.

Although they tend to be needed only rarely, forceps should be in every good carp angler's kit. When a hook has hit bone or is really awkwardly positioned in the mouth finger and thumb sometimes can't exert enough direct pressure. Forceps carefully clamped around the bend or shank and then used to pull a hook back out the way it came will extract even the most stubborn hooks thanks to increased leverage. The smaller of the forceps in the Fox Predator range double perfectly for extracting buried carp hooks.

Fox Predator Forceps (PTL006). Perfect for the job!

A small pair of wire cutters available from any DIY store are also a responsible addition to your carp care kit. Very, very occasionally you might encounter a hook that has buried then come out the other side of a carp's mouth. Although incredibly rare thanks to modern rig efficiency a hook that has taken hold this way is best snipped into two pieces using wire cutters rather than pulled all the way back through. You might only ever need wire cutters a handful of times in many years carping, but you'll be very thankful to have them on those few occasions, whether for safely unhooking your own carp or one that someone else is struggling with.

Fox Predator Extra Long Side Cutters (PTL005) are perfect for cutting hooks - carry them just in case.

ANTISEPTIC TREATMENTS

CARP suffer knocks and bangs in day to day life, whether accidental such as from the frenzy of summer spawning or angler related from poor bankside care.

It's responsible and highly recommended to carry antiseptic to treat fish displaying signs of damage and there are a number of treatments commercially available to help carp recover from cuts, sores and body wounds. If everybody carried and used antiseptics we would quickly see carp in much better condition day to day on many venues.

Some antiseptics are better than others. The two used and recommended by the Fox Carp Team are Bonjela and Orabase Protective Paste. Both are antiseptic gels used for the treatment of mouth ulcers and other minor injuries in humans. Being gels rather than liquids they have the advantage that they don't wash off after application as soon as a fish is returned. A generous smear applied around lifted scales or fresh hook damage will help disinfect the wound and promote healing and fresh tissue growth. Orabase contains a growth promoting steroid that has been seen to work wonders when fish have been caught quickly again after treatment. Both Bonjela and Orabase are widely available from any high street chemists or supermarket pharmacy.

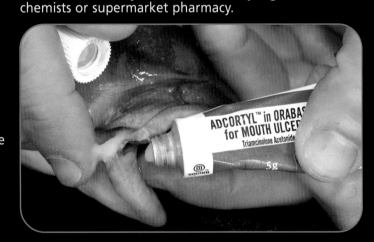

Some antiseptics are better than others. The Fox Carp Team recommend Bonjela and Orabase protective paste.

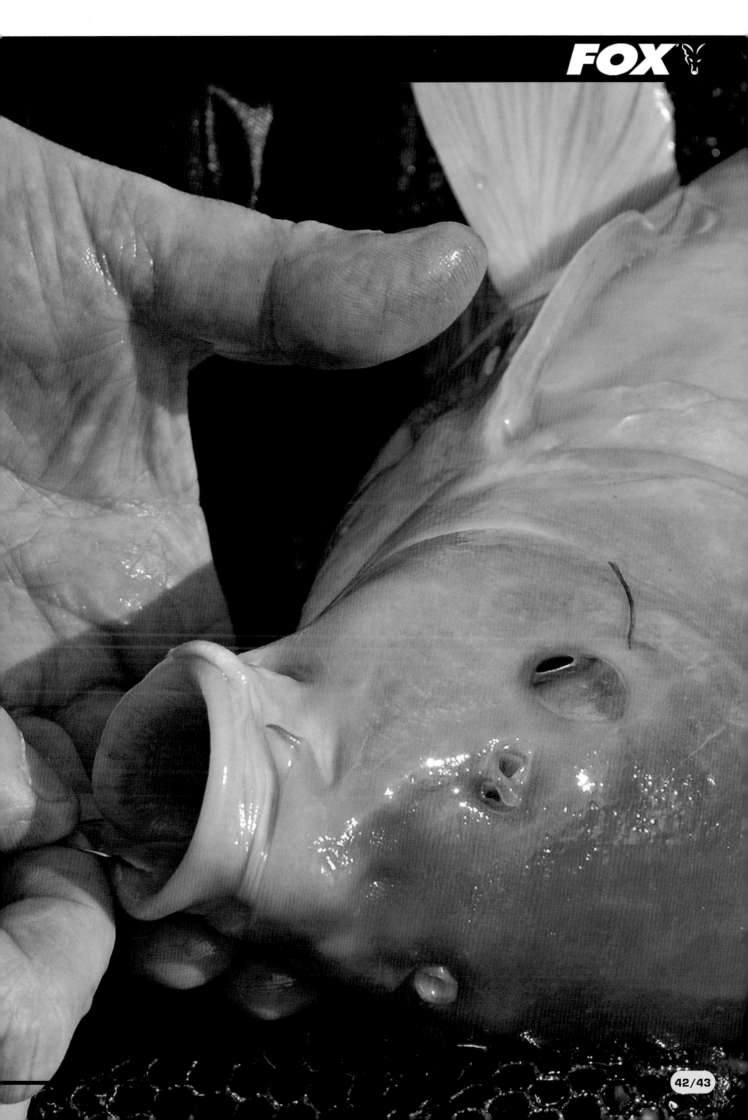

WEIGHING AND RETURNING

ACCURATE weighing records your achievements with personal best fish as you progress in carp angling, and also helps indicate growth rates of carp in a fishery. With the right kit and good practice consistent weighing is a straight forward procedure.

UNBEATABLE FOR ACCURACY

FOX digital scales have set new standards for accuracy and consistency when weighing specimen fish. Where traditional dial scales are based around the performance of springs that can vary in accuracy with age and loading, Fox digital models use a high quality electronic chassis for unrivalled reliability.

When used to weigh the 19 lb 10 oz record bream Fox Digital Scales were independently tested by Peterborough Trading Standards at 14 different weights, proving to be 100 per cent accurate across all readings - testimony in itself to the unbeatable performance of top quality electronics for reliable weighing.

The former record chub of 9 lb 3 oz caught by Steve White was weighed on digital scales with the same result – their accuracy was bang on when independently tested by Weights and Measures officials. The accuracy of Fox digital scales has also been acknowledged by the British Record Fish Committee.

The new Stalker Scales offer the same digital accuracy from a tough weighing chassis in a compact, lightweight body. Folding handles and retractable weighing eye allow the Stalker Scales to be slipped neatly into the smallest rucksacks or carryalls, weighing up to 55lb in 1 oz divisions. The reading can also be changed from pounds to kilos or to Dutch pounds at the push of a button. An optional hard case protects the Stalkers from accidental damage in transit between sessions.

Fox's Digital Scales boast a huge range of features including push button operation, easy to read LCD display with backlighting for night time work, built in clock and catch record memory facility, clip on protective hard case, and are available in black finish or Advantage Timber camouflage.

"Every set of Fox digital scales we have had tested for a record fish claim have come out spot on"

Gary Newman Angler's Mail reporter

WEIGHING

1. You can weigh carp in nets or sling style unhooking mats but it's best to use a purpose designed weigh sling. This is the Safety Weigh Sling.

2. After wetting the sling thoroughly allow excess water to drain off. Suspend the sling on the scales and zero the sling in using the Zero or 0.00 button.

3. Place the pre-zeroed sling on the mat next to the carp, then lift the carp off the net and unhooking mat and into the sling, ensuring the sides are zipped up.

4. Suspend the sling on the scales and lift the scales using the two fold out handles. Hold the scales steady until the display settles on a weight.

5. For heavier fish that can be difficult to hold for any period of time the Fox weighing handle and pole allows you to lift and suspend the scales and carp absolutely steady with very little effort.

6. After weighing and photographing carp should always be returned to the water's edge in a sling or mat. Never carry carp in your arms - one flip and they are out of your grip and can land on their heads. Unzip the sides of the Safety Weigh Sling and flood water over the sling, allowing the carp to slide off and out back into the lake. Keep a carp supported in the sling until it kicks its tail and swims away strongly.

7. With mats like the Carp Cradle float them out into the margins then sink the leading edge to flood water over the mat. The carp will slip off and kick away as the mat floods.

HEARN - LANE - LOCKE -
SHARP - CLARKE - REGAN -
SPRINGATE - PAGULATOS -
HAYWARD - ROMP - WOODS -
CROW - FAIRBRASS - READ -
FARNHAM - COTTAM - HUGHES -
MCALLISTER - DORSETT -
HAMIDI - MOORS - WRIGHT -
MOFFAT - MORGAN - SCOTT -
LYTHGOE - NASH - SYKES -
BAKER - PENNING - GERALDINE.

IN ALL LEADING RETAILERS.

CHAPTER 3
END TACKLES

BEHIND THE LEAD
TUBING, LEAD CORE AND LEADERS

IT'S rare to see a carp end tackle without a couple of feet of a semi-stiff leader material behind the rig, whether a pre-formed looped nylon leader, a length of anti-tangle tubing or a section of lead core line.

Tubing, lead core and leaders have multiple functions, the first and arguably the most important being to improve the anti-tangle properties of a rig. Since the 80s when plastic tubing was first used up the line it has been accepted that any higher diameter, semi-stiff material behind the lead will prevent supple hook lengths from tangling with the main line during the cast. As long as the length of the tubing, lead core or leader being used exceeds the length of the hook length by around 10cm tangles will be effectively eliminated. Preventing tangles is absolutely fundamental to effective carp fishing. There is nothing as disappointing as discovering you have been sitting behind rods with tangled rigs for hours or even overnight with no chance of a take.

Leaders also protect carp from line damage when using braided reel lines. A low diameter braided line under tension is as dangerous to a carp as it is to your finger when casting. Braids can lift scales, damage the dorsal fin or even in extreme circumstances cut into the body of a carp during the fight. Long three foot or more leaders protect the carp by preventing the braid contacting the fish, although there is no danger when using mono reel lines without leaders.

The last few feet of line behind a rig is the section that takes the majority of wear and tear from catching fish, and always the most likely to be rubbed up against snags or sharp flints and stones during a fight. Any leader material improves abrasion resistance of the last few feet of an end tackle, reducing chances of tackle loss or failure through damage.

Lastly, and of key importance in today's world of pressurised carp venues is camouflage and line concealment. Leaders help pin your line down to the lake bed and conceal it from wary carp, breaking up or camouflaging a continuous line that might otherwise give away the presence of an end tackle.

WHICH LEADER?
IN the same way carpers develop their own preferences for lines, hook patterns, successful rigs and even baiting techniques, the carp world is split between fans of lead core leaders, nylon leaders and anti-tangle tubing. Fox consultant Ian Chillcott would feel as if he'd had his right arm taken away fishing without lead core such is his confidence in it, yet Andy Little and Colin Davidson routinely rig up for carp with nothing other than a lead, swivel and hook length for end tackle, choosing not to use any leader material of any description. Different leaders have different properties but all effectively perform the same tasks. Personal preference as often as practicality dictates which one you use.

ANTI-TANGLE TUBING
TUBING has come a long way since the shiny, high diameter black plastic lengths of tube of yesteryear. Fox's tinted rig tube threads easily, sinks, offers tremendous abrasion resistance and sits unobtrusively over any lake bed thanks to its natural debris colour finish.

Although now less fashionable than lead core or the new breed of pre-formed nylon leaders tubing is still an essential item of terminal tackle for the travelling carper. Although an area for much debate, numbers of venues have banned both lead core and nylon leaders in the interests of protecting their stocks against possible dangers from lost end tackles, leaving anti-tangle tubing one of the best ways to minimise tangles.

TUBING TIPS

1. Main line should be clean, straight and cut to a point with sharp scissors before being threaded down anti-tangle tubing.

2. The tubing should be clean, dry and straight. Always thread line downwards. It's simple but gravity is a big help. If the line sticks try twisting from side to side as you push down.

3. Cut your length of anti-tangle tubing, then gently pull it straight between the fingers to remove any coiling memory from storage. Line is much easier to thread down straight lengths of tubing.

4. Cutting the tubing to a point helps threading rig components like safety clips, beads and tail rubbers on.

TUNGSTEN LOADED TUBING

FOR lead core fans tackling venues where their favourite leader material is banned, Fox loaded tungsten rig tube is the perfect solution. Impregnating dense tungsten particles into PVA anti-tangle tubing as it is extruded creates an incredibly heavy tubing that sinks quickly and hugs the lake bed in exactly the same way as a lead core leader.

TOP TIP
Tungsten loaded rig tube has a number of applications for the thinking carper, such as adding weight to improve hooking with light lead end tackles yet still allowing them to be cast with the minimum of disturbance when in front of feeding fish.

"Semi-stiff leader material offer many functions, arguably the most important being to improve the anti-tangle properties of a rig"

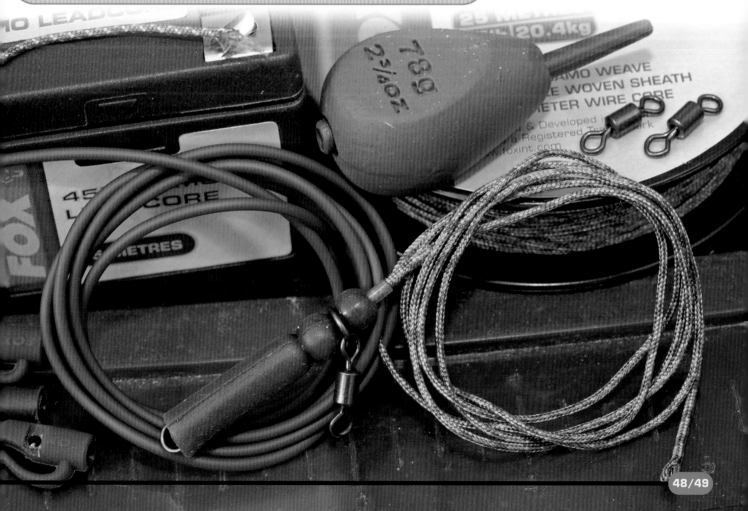

LEAD CORE

USED since the early 90s lead core line has found favour amongst carp anglers thanks to its high abrasion resistance and ability to sink and help conceal line. Characterised by a robust woven polyester outer with a fine, flexible lead wire inner, lead core lines soak up the day to day punishment of knocks and scrapes against gravel, thick weed or snags making them a perfect leader choice. Lower diameter than anti-tangle tubing, lead core casts further and more smoothly than tubing end tackles, is highly camouflaged thanks to the woven, fleck finish of the polyester outer and sinks quickly to pin the last few feet of your end tackle down away from the eyes and fins of wary carp.

Fox lead core has been carefully designed with a lighter coloured, more complex polyester outer weave, experience showing that this finish offers maximum concealment over gravel, clay or sand where other lead core lines clearly show as dark continuous lines when immersed in water. Rated at 45 lb it features a high density lead wire inner for fast sinking and is supplied with a splicing needle for easy end tackle construction.

HOW MUCH?

THERE is no right or wrong answer as to how much lead core to use for a leader. Some experienced carpers have found success with leaders as long as six or eight feet, feeling that pinning as much line down to the lake bed as possible is advantageous. Remember though that lead core is semi-stiff rather than a supple material, and will not necessarily lie along the lake bed if there are small undulations, large stones or steep changes of depth behind bars and drop-offs.

More commonly leaders of 18 inches to three feet offer sufficient length for effective anti-tangle properties, and pin down and camouflage the line in the immediate vicinity of the rig. Fox lead core is available on five metre dispensers to fit F and System Fox Boxes or 25 metre spools for the regular user who prefers to tie or splice their own longer leaders.

SPLICING LEAD CORE

THERE are several ways to attach lead core end lengths to reel lines. The easiest method is to splice a loop on the end of a length of lead core and then tie the line to it in the same way you would tie the reel line to a swivel or eyed hook. A splice works on constriction, trapping material within itself so it grips itself when under pressure. Spliced loops are tough, reliable and with practice very easy to construct.

1. To splice loops we need to remove around 6-8cm of lead wire from inside the lead core. Pull the polyester outer back and then snip off the lead.

5. Hold the section of the leader where the needle passes through the centre of the polyester between finger and thumb and gently pull the needle trapping the end of the lead core back through it.

"Spliced loops are tough, reliable and with practice very easy to construct"

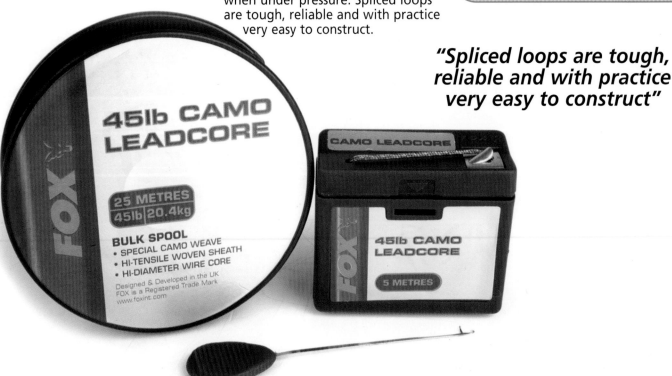

HOW TO SPLICE A LOOP IN LEAD CORE

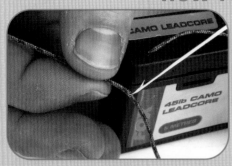

2. Fox lead core is supplied with a low diameter splicing needle with a lip close end. Where the lead ends and the inside of the lead core is now hollow push the splicing needle into the centre of the polyester sheath.

3. Push the needle 1.5-2cm down the centre of the polyester outer and then push the needle back out through the side of the polyester.

4. Trim the very end of the lead core so the woven fibres are neat rather than splayed loosely. Insert the end of the lead core into the splicing needle and close the lip to secure it.

6. Once the needle emerges keep pulling the tag end until you begin to form a small loop at the end of the length of lead core. Keep tightening until the loop is around 5mm.

7. Now carefully trim the excess lead core tag end where it exits the polyester outer. Snip tight up against the lead core, the splice will not slip at all.

8. To create the other end of the leader repeat the process, threading a ring swivel on the lead core after the lead inner is removed and before the splice is formed. Rig bits such as safety clips, rubbers or beads can be threaded on the leader from the spliced loop end.

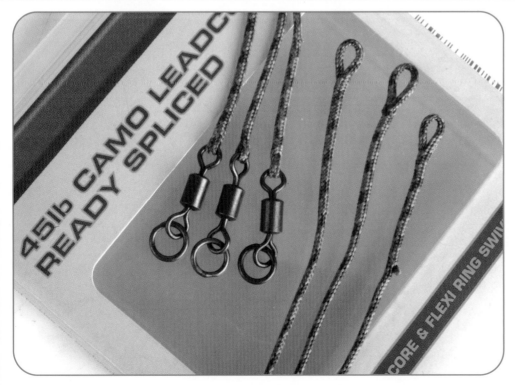

If you find splicing tricky Fox ready spliced lead core leaders are supplied with ring swivels at one end and a spliced loop at the other for easy attachment. Just slide on your rig components or an in-line lead, knot the spliced loop to the main line and you're ready to go.

TOP TIP
Attach your lead core leader to the main line with a five turn grinner knot or a Palomar knot to the spliced loop, exactly as you would tie line to a swivel or hook.

LEADS

It has never been more critical to understand the importance of choosing the right lead.

Responsible for so much more than casting weight in a modern carp rig, lead choice is fundamental to rig efficiency, influencing everything from how effectively you can present baits in different swims and conditions to how likely you are to land the carp you have hooked.

The Fox range of carp leads are designed using CAD engineering ensuring optimum aerodynamics for longer casting and improved hooking efficiency to convert more pick ups to runs. Precision injection moulding provides absolute consistency of performance, with a range that covers every application from light lead small water work on pressurised UK fisheries to anchoring rigs hundreds of metres out in the largest inland seas of the Continent.

SWIVEL LEADS

Fox swivel leads are fitted with large eye rubber coated swivels and enlarged loops. All Fox leads have a special non-reflective rubberised coating which improves the durability of the lead when used on gravel. Swivels can be removed for improved anti-tangle performance and bolt effect with Fox safety clips.

IN-LINE LEADS

Fox in-line leads are fitted with integral safety sleeves designed to take a size 7 swivel. If the lead gets snagged it will pull free from the sleeve unlike other in-line systems where the swivel is locked and must be pulled free from inside the lead. Turn over to see how Fox in-line safety sleeves work.

IN-LINE SAFETY SLEEVE

Fish safety is the number one priority at Fox. Our Inline leads have been designed to create rigs that are completely safe. All the leads have a wide bore into which a Rubber safety sleeve fits. In the event of a break in the mainline, the safety sleeve will pull free from a tethered lead freeing the carp.

1. A size 7 swivel secures the lead on the line.

2. If the lead becomes snagged the safety sleeve will start to pull through.

3. The large bore of the lead means leaders pass through unhindered.

4. Most importantly, the bore is big enough to allow loops in leadcore to sail through it.

HORIZON

FLAT PEAR

PASTE BOMBS

HORIZON LEADS

The classic aerodynamic bomb for extreme distance casting, the smoothly tapered weight forward design provides tremendous accuracy and stability in flight, even in crosswinds while the six sided profile prevents rolling to maintain hooking efficiency.

The slender design of the Horizon ensures smooth, quiet entry into the water, making the smaller sizes valuable on pressurised smaller venues to minimise disturbance when rigs are being positioned.

Swivels can be snipped off, making the Horizon leads tangle-free with safety clips for long to extreme range casting.

Minus the swivel Horizon leads can be added to Speed Links for neat quick change helicopter end tackles on lead core.

FLAT PEAR LEADS

The tapered shape of the Flat Pear makes it one of the most versatile lead designs ever produced.

As an in-line the weight forward, flattened profile ensures maximum bolt effect when hook lengths are tightened, pulling hook points in more efficiently than more slender bomb shapes.

Flat pears also prevent end tackles rolling from marginal slopes or bars, keeping them anchored in position to intercept patrolling carp.

The swivel Flat Pear is ideal for running rigs, its shape ensuring it remains in position on the lake bed rather than rolling or bouncing on the take - ensuring line is freely pulled through the swivel for effective indication.

In-line 2-3 oz Flat Pears are ideal with short 6-10cm braided links for tucking inside solid PVA bags loaded with pellet and chopped boilies. Swivel Flat Pears of 1.5 to 2.5 oz make effective running rigs for the best indication possible at short to medium range.

PASTE BOMBS

Unique to Fox the Paste Bombs can be used as a standard lead or have bait moulded around them. The CAD generated shape features slimline recesses that grip Method mixes or balls of pastes to enhance attraction around the hook bait.

Aerodynamic and long casting thanks to their rounded shape, the fluted profile also ensures the Paste Bombs rise quickly to the surface on the retrieve making them ideal for snaggy and weedy waters.

Method mixes like Vitalin or softened pellet mould securely around the Paste Bombs.

The largest Paste Bombs when loaded with bait can weigh 5-6 oz, so strong 15-20 lb main lines are required and casting should be limited to short ranges.

KLING ON

TRI-BOMB

ELEVATOR

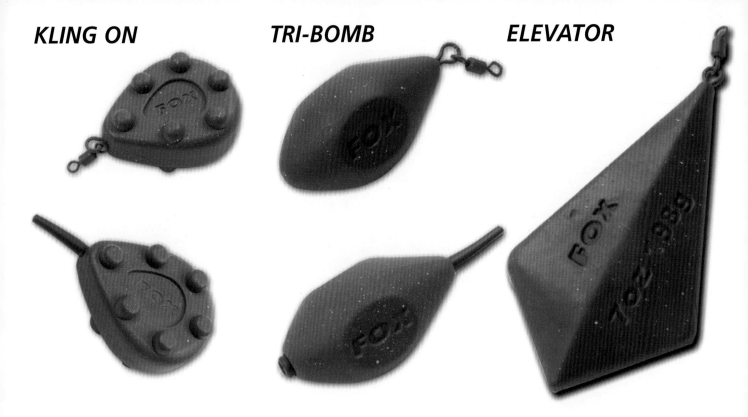

KLING ON LEADS

Another unique design to Fox, the Kling On features both top and bottom surfaces textured with pronounced studs to improve grip on any type of bottom, whether in flowing or tidal venues or when needing to nail hook baits to steeply sloping island margins and bars. The flattened, compact profile prevents rigs rolling and maximises bolt effect.

Kling Ons are the perfect choice when positioning hook baits from a boat or remote boat, improving grip and bolt effect.

TRI-BOMB LEADS

Suitable for a huge number of applications, the Tri-Bomb's are a great allround lead. The three sided shape is aerodynamic enough to be cast long distances, yet the flattened, compact shape concentrates weight to prevent rolling on sloping or uneven lake beds and improves hooking efficiency with both running and semi-fixed end tackles.

Tri-Bomb in-lines are versatile enough to use over gravel or silt and offer effective hooking.

ELEVATOR LEADS

The distinctive three sided shape of the Elevator is designed to aqua plane the lead up quickly through the water on the retrieve, reducing the chances of snagging underwater obstacles like thick weed or snags or damaging rigs on large gravel features. Aerodynamic enough for long casting, but also ideal for boating rigs out long distances, Continental style.

Elevators rise up over snags and weed on the retrieve to prevent tackle loss.

Increased contact with the lake bed through the Kling On's studs nails hook baits even on steeply sloping shelves or bars.

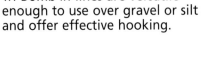

Use swivel Tri-Bombs on safety clips for improved bolt effect at medium to long range.

The three sided shape also makes them ideal for holding position in flowing water.

"Lead choice is fundamental to rig efficiency"

IN-LINE LEADS

IN-LINE leads are leads that we thread the main line through and were originally developed to reduce tangles through being more streamlined than leads that hung down away from the line.

Hook length swivels are pulled into an insert through the centre of an in-line lead to semi-fix them. Because the swivel is fixed to the centre of the heaviest end of the lead carp tightening the hook length instantly feel maximum resistance, helping drive a hook home efficiently. Compared to other lead arrangements in-liners - particularly dumpy designs - create maximum bolt effect for a given lead size. When tackling wary carp, any improvement in hooking efficiency can result in significantly improved catches, making in-line leads understandably popular.

But the position that the hook length swivel is joined to the lead also brings drawbacks. In-liners don't cast as well as swivel lead designs because the resistance of the hook bait in flight is always pulling directly at the nose of the lead, making them much less effective for longer range casting. Heavier in-lines can also sit nose down as they land which can lead to poor presentation over hard and soft bottoms, especially with stiff and semi-stiff presentations.

TOP TIP
In-lines provide the best hooking over hard bottoms such as clay, gravel or sand, maximising bolt effect.

WHEN AND WHERE

✓ IN THE MARGINS
In-line leads offer a maximum bolt effect when a hook length is tightened, and are perfect for margin or stalking traps where rigs are gently lowered or swung in.

✓ INSIDE SOLID PVA BAGS
In-lines are ideal to tuck neatly into solid PVA bags and compress the feed tightly around, helping to hide your lead and rig.

✓ WITH PVA STICK RIGS
Lighter 1.5 to 2.5 oz in-line leads with a Kwik Change Swivel pushed into the rubber insert are ideal end tackles to use with PVA sticks threaded up a hook length.

TYING AN IN-LINE RIG

1. In-line leads can be used with lead core, nylon leaders or anti-tangle tubing behind the lead to reduce tangles, conceal and pin the main line down. Here we are threading a Flat Pear in-line on a ready spliced lead core leader using a stringer needle.

2. A size 7 Fox swivel is designed to fit perfectly inside the rubber sleeve insert of all Fox in-line leads. It's important always to use the right size swivel.

3. Carp safety is paramount, and all Fox in-line leads are designed to pull free of the rubber insert that grips the size 7 swivel if the lead becomes jammed in weed or snags.

4. Because the lead releases from the insert, the large bore of the lead then easily passes over leaders and spliced loops of lead core to prevent any chance of a carp towing a lead in the event of a main line breakage.

RUNNING LEADS

ONE of the simplest but most versatile end tackles of all running rigs are largely neglected in favour of semi-fixed leads. With much rig theory revolving around the need for a fixed point of resistance to pull a hook home when the hook length tightens many lack the confidence to use a running rig.

But the weight and tension of the main line and even indicator arrangement at the rods is enough to pressure a hook point in when a carp picks up the hook bait with a running rig. Takes are as fast and furious with running rigs as they are with heavy semi-fixed leads.

Running rigs also show up small pulls from carp or nuisance fish picking up the hook bait far more readily than any semi-fixed lead end tackle. Because the lead can easily slide straight off the line in event of breakage a running rig is also the safest end tackle.

Running rigs are considered a great help catching wary carp that routinely use the fixed resistance of a semi-fixed lead to shake their head and bounce a hook out the mouth. It is often the bigger fish that use this tactic.

Line running freely through a lead makes it very difficult for carp to shake a hook free once it has gained an initial hold.

With different size and shape leads and different lengths of hook length and bait choice running rigs will present baits effectively over anything but thick weed.

Running rigs can be tied with either lead core and anti-tangle tubing and indication will be superior to end tackles using semi-fixed leads but simple is best and line runs most smoothly and indication at its best when leads are threaded straight on to nylon or fluorocarbon main line.

WHEN AND WHERE

For very pressurised carp Running rigs perform brilliantly where carp are used to heavy semi-fixed end tackles such as in-liners or safety clips, bringing improved results.

✓ SNAG FISHING
Instant indication from a running rig is also beneficial when fishing locked up close to snags. In the event of a breakage a running rig also offers improved rig safety.

✓ IN THE WINTER
In colder temperatures running rigs maximise indication, helping register takes from carp that are feeding very slowly and may not give spool spinning takes.

✓ WITH SHOCK/SNAG LEADERS
Whenever there is a knot behind the end tackle joining a snag or shock leader to the main line a running lead improves rig safety in the event of breakages.

TYING A RUNNING RIG

1. Thread a 1.5-3 oz Flat Pear lead up the main line followed by a knot protector bead.

2. Tie a size 7 ring swivel on with a Palomar or five turn grinner knot.

3. Push the knot protector bead over the barrel of the swivel then tie the hook length to the ring swivel.

4. As long as you can cast the required distance, stick to dumpy lead designs like the Tri-Bomb or Flat Pear for optimum performance with running rigs.

5. With combi-links like Coretex, mono or fluorocarbon hook lengths running rigs are reliably tangle free without any tubing or lead core.

6. A stringer or cobweb PVA bag nicked on to the hook before casting guarantees no chance of tangles even with soft, braided hook lengths.

"Running rigs perform brilliantly where carp are used to heavy semi-fixed end tackles"

1. Remove a section of inner wire and splice a 5mm loop at one end of the camo lead core.

5. Attach your chosen lead size and shape to the Speed Link then push the bead and sleeve down tightly over the top of the link and lead swivel. The ring swivel and bead will sit just above it.

HELICOPTER RIGS

Helicopter rigs are loved by some and disliked by others. No other end tackle attracts such fiercely opposed viewpoints.

To construct a helicopter rig leads are tied directly to the end of the line or leader, the hook length tied to a swivel revolving freely on the leader, tubing or main line between stop beads back up behind the lead. The helicopter rig is an incredibly long casting end tackle, the hook length and bait revolving like a helicopter's blades at 90 degrees to the main line, guaranteeing tangle free presentation even at long distances. But there are safety issues with helicopter rigs, both for anglers and carp.

When tied with anti-tangle tubing, repeated scraps with carp on helicopter rigs were found to lead to the ring swivel cutting through the tubing and into the main line it revolved around. Of course, this had the potential to cause a breakage, particularly with lighter breaking strain main lines.

If using tubing it is essential to stick to main lines of 15 lb breaking strain, and inspect the line where it is tied to the lead to check for signs of wear or damage. The universal adoption of tough lead core leaders has also largely solved the main line breakage problems associated with helicopter rigs.

There are however concerns about the safety of lead core helicopter rigs. Badly constructed helicopter rigs can be potentially lethal to carp. In the event of line breakage the hook length swivel on a badly constructed helicopter rig will not be able to freely slide up the lead core and over the leader knot or spliced loop to rid the carp of the end tackle. A carp towing a lead on a length of high breaking strain, abrasion resistant lead core can easily become tethered.

Fans of helicopter rigs argue that a well constructed helicopter rig is safer than most other end tackles because in the event of a breakage a carp is only left towing the hook length which is quickly discarded. Critics point out that there are too many examples where inexperienced carp anglers are using badly constructed and potentially dangerous helicopter rigs, and some fisheries have banned lead core and helicopter rigs on this basis.

TYING A HELICOPTER RIG

The Fox Heli Kit contains all the components to construct a safe helicopter rig on lead core or tubing.

2. At the other end splice a Speed Link, keeping the length of lead core leader no more than 30cm.

3. Thread the rubber shock bead, ring swivel and the specially designed bead and sleeve on to a lip close baiting needle. The needle must be passing through the ring of the swivel NOT the eye.

4. Locate the needle in the spliced loop at the end of the leader and push all the rig components on to the lead core leader.

6. Cut a 5 to 10mm section of the silicone tube and thread it over the spliced loop and down the lead core. Lubricating with saliva helps it slide. Position the silicone 1-2cm above the bead and sleeve.

7. Push and twist the top rubber bead over the silicone tube to fix it in position. Tie your hook length to the swivel, checking it rotates freely between the top bead and the bead and sleeve.

8. To check the rig is safe hold the lead and pull the hook length up the lead core against the stop bead and silicone tube. The bead should slide over the silicone, allowing the hook length to freely slide off the lead core.

The smallest detail in terms of rig bits and construction can change a safe effective end tackle into a lethal one, and never is this more clearly illustrated than with the helicopter rig.

Helicopter rigs have a role in the modern carp angler's armoury but they must be used with greater care than more simple rigs like running leads and in-line rigs. Spend time perfecting your helicopter rig to ensure it is carp-friendly.

Fox has spent a huge amount of time and money developing its helicopter accessories and ready assembled helicopter rigs.

All products have been carefully researched and constructed with meticulous detail to ensure a carp's safety at all times, particularly in the event of unexpected main line breakage, guaranteeing that should you need to use a helicopter rig you can be confident that you are doing so safely.

HELICOPTERS OFF THE SHELF

CONVENIENT and offering absolute peace of mind over carp safety Fox supply three styles of ready assembled helicopter rigs straight out of the packet.

Lead Core Heli Rigs are constructed from the same rig components contained in the Heli Kit, mounted on 45 lb camo lead core with a spliced loop for easy attachment to your main line and Speed Links for easy lead changes.

The same components are also supplied on Fox tinted camo tubing for use on venues where lead core is banned.

For maximum efficiency Fox now supply identical helicopter rigs mounted on lead core using Kwik Change Swivels and Sleeves that allow looped hook lengths to be replaced in seconds. All Fox ready tied helicopter end tackles are supplied in threes.

WHEN AND WHERE

✓ OVER SOFT BOTTOMS

The helicopter rig allows heavy leads to be fished in soft silt but the hook length is pushed back up the line so it settles on top of silt rather than being dragged down into it.

✓ WITH STIFF LINKS

Stiff hook lengths have to be presented flat over the lake bed to work effectively. The helicopter rig lays a stiff rig out behind it as the lead lands for perfect presentation.

✓ LONG RANGE FISHING

Although not recommended with shock leaders the helicopter rig is incredibly aerodynamic for long casting because the bomb is effectively tied direct to the end of the line.

✓ WITH THE CHOD RIG

A vogue presentation the chod rig is a short stiff hook length presenting a pop-up hook bait directly off a length of lead core. It has to be fished on a helicopter end tackle to work effectively.

SAFETY CLIPS

ORIGINALLY adapted from small clips used to mount swimfeeders by match and pleasure anglers safety clips allow leads to be mounted on end tackles for virtually tangle free casting, with the added benefit that leads can be jettisoned to improve rig safety. They are a tremendously popular and versatile lead mounting arrangement.

Safety clips slide over hook length swivels with the lead held on a small retaining lug underneath the body of the clip. A soft tapered sleeve or tail rubber is pushed over the clip to prevent the lead from coming free.

There are numbers of benefits of safety clip systems. They allow the size and shape of a lead to be altered in seconds for different venues, swims or conditions. More importantly lead clips allow us to fish more safely in snaggy and weedy swims. It's almost always the lead that becomes stuck when carp are snagged or weeded.

Because the lead is mounted on the retaining lug rather than directly on the line or leader any build up of pressure on the lead causes the tail rubber to slide off the clip. With no lead we are left with a direct line to a carp to exert increased pressure, there's no tackle hanging from the line to jam up.

With the weight released from the line carp also fight close to or on the surface making them easier to control and land in weedy and snaggy swims. Safety clips also allow leads to be removed from made-up rods between sessions or when moving swims, preventing damage to expensive blanks or varnish.

Unfortunately safety clips can easily be set up incorrectly, in extreme cases becoming potentially dangerous. For a safety clip to work effectively the clip must be firmly anchored to the hook length swivel so any build up of pressure can only force the lead from the retaining lug. Fox Safety Lead Clips feature a removable peg that lock them to the eye of hook length swivels for reliable performance.

WHEN AND WHERE

✓ IN WEEDY VENUES
When carp become bogged down in weed it is the lead that is often jammed up. Pressure on the lead causes it to pop off a clip allowing carp to be more easily landed.

✓ FOR LONG RANGE FISHING
A safety clip with a distance lead design is a long and accurate casting end tackle. Because the lead isn't mounted on the line and can easily be jettisoned safety clip end tackles offer improved safety with shock leaders.

✓ TO IMPROVE VERSATILITY
When visiting new venues or where a venue presents changing conditions and vastly differing swims lead clips allow you to change the size and shape of leads to suit weed, distance fishing, silt or gravel bottoms in seconds.

✗ NOT WITH PVA BAGS
Unless the end tackle is feathered on impact a cobweb PVA bag hitting the surface of the water and tightening the hook length can bounce the lead from the retaining lug of a safety clip every cast. Stick to running and in-line rigs with cobweb bags.

1. Safety clips can be used direct on the main line, with anti-tangle tubing or with lead core leaders. Here we're using a Fox ready spliced lead core leader complete with ring swivel.

2. Using a stringer needle thread the clip followed by the tail rubber on to the lead core leader over the spliced loop.

3. Pull the ring swivel into the body of the clip. Fox clips are designed so when the swivel is pulled as far as it will go the eye is perfectly in position to accept the peg.

4. The peg is pushed into the hole until it clicks and is flush with the body of the clip. Slide a lead on top the retaining lug and then push the tail rubber over the rear of the clip. Tie your hook length to the ring of the ring swivel and the end tackle is ready to use.

RIGHT AND WRONG

Grip the lead and pull the hook length. If the clip remains anchored and the lead is pulled off the retaining lug the clip is set up safely. If the clip separates from the swivel it is not a safely constructed end tackle.

TOP TIP

SWIVELS can be removed from Fox leads with wire cutters, sitting the leads tighter to the clip, removing a potential tangle point and improving hooking. Dumpy leads offer greater resistance when carp tighten the hook length - bringing more takes.

KNOTS

AN end tackle is only as strong as its weakest link. Strong, reliable knots are an essential feature of any discipline of angling. But the sheer power a hooked carp displays will reveal any shortcomings in your knot tying sooner rather than later.

GRINNER KNOT

ARGUABLY the most versatile knot of all, the Grinner knot can be used for virtually every job in modern carp angling. Invented by the late Richard Walker, and commonly referred to as the Uni Knot it offers strength and reliability with all materials from mono to fluorocarbon, braids and coated links.

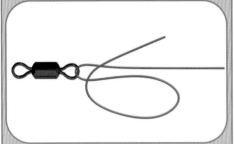

1. Thread the line through the swivel or hook and turn it back on itself to form a loop.

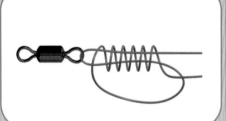

2. Pass the tag end around the main line and through the loop five times.

3. Lubricate with saliva and pull the tag end gently to tighten until the knot is a neat barrel.

4. Hold the main line and slide the knot barrel between finger and thumb until tight to the swivel. Trim the tag end to 2-3mm.

PALOMAR KNOT

LIKE the Grinner the Palomar is a versatile knot that can be used for tying line to any rig bits, maintaining maxium knot strength. Excellent for tying main lines to spliced lead core loops or loops in fused nylon leaders because of the small, streamlined finish to the knot that allows rig bits to pass easily over it.

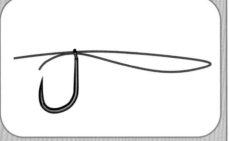

1. Double a length of line 8-10cm long. Push the apex of the doubled line through the eye.

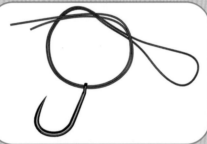

2. Turn the doubled line back on itself and pass the apex through the loop formed.

3. Push the hook or swivel between the strands at the apex of the doubled line.

4. Lubricate with saliva and gently pull both tag end and main line together to tighten down.

FIGURE OF EIGHT KNOT

MUCH stronger than the commonly used overhand loop the figure of eight knot is best used for heavier breaking strain fluorocarbon links, boom sections of combi-links and coated hook length materials like Coretex. Traces tied with figure of eight loops slip easily into kwik change swivels for easy replacement.

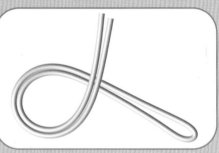

1. Double a length of line 8-10cm long and fold it back on itself.

2. Pull the apex of the doubled line upwards.

3. Pull it back round behind the loop before feeding it through. Lubricate with saliva.

4. You see the distinctive figure of eight shape as the knot is drawn tight.

THREE TURN BLOOD KNOT

ALTHOUGH less reliable when used with braids, mono and fluorocarbon the three turn blood knot is another useful knot for stiff link materials, the tag end tightened to form the finished knot rather than main line. Again, blobbing the tag end with a lighter improves security.

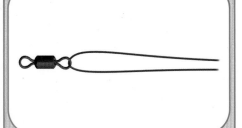

1. Pass the line through the eye of a swivel or hook.

2. Wrap the tag end around the main line three times.

3. Pass the tag end through the hole formed between the swivel and first turn.

4. Lubricate with saliva and tighten by pulling the tag end.

RIGIDITY KNOT

INCREDIBLY simple the Rigidity knot is perfect for tying stiff materials like Fox Rigidity, keeping links short, straight and strong. Blobbing the tag end after tightening improves knot security.

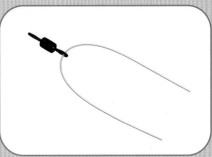

1. Pass the length of Rigidity through the eye.

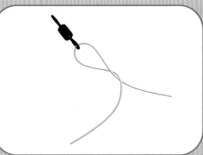

2. Wrap the tag end once around the main line.

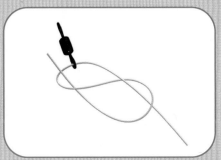

3. Pass the tag end behind the loop and then pass it through.

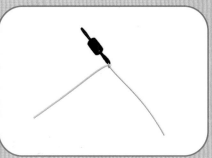

4. Lubricate with saliva then pull the tag end to tighten.

5. Pull the tag end at 90 degrees to main line, trim, then carefully blob with a lighter.

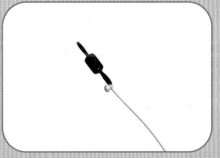

6. Push a wet finger tip over the tag end to flatten the tag end for security.

TOP TIP

LUBRICATING any knot with saliva as it is drawn tight reduces friction, prevents heat build up and results in a stronger knot. Always test your knots before casting out. The Fox Tension Bar is ideal for pulling against swivels or hooks to bed knots down tightly and check they are secure.

STIFF LINK KNOTS

MATERIALS that have an inherent stiffness can't easily be tied with many common knots. Knots that are tightened down using the tag end only prevent curling of a stiff link or lengthening of presentations that are intended to be kept short for optimum hooking efficiency like the Chod Rig.

OTHER KNOTS:
Shockleader Knot P84-85
Hair Loop P182
Splicing Lead Core P50-51

CHAPTER 4
LINES

LINES

FROM the days where virtually every single carp reel was filled with one of two major brands of monofilament, carp and specialist lines have undergone dramatic development. Now tackle shop shelves are filled with huge numbers of different lines, all with different properties and designed for different jobs. You'll find a range of materials, colours, breaking strains, floating and sinking lines, camouflaged lines, the choice is vast. So which lines are best and what for?

FLUOROCARBON

The most recent addition to the carp angler's armoury of main lines fluorocarbon offers tremendous tactical advantages to your end tackle set up.

Originally used as a tippet material for wary trout by fly fishermen, fluorocarbon has a light refractive index very close to that of water which makes it virtually invisible. Most fish species have very keen eyesight and a line less visible in water often brings more action helping fool wary fish.

In big game fishing fluorocarbon traces can bring as many as ten times more strikes at baits than those fished on mono links. But carp aren't sight feeding predators and we are using fluorocarbon as a main line not necessarily as a hook length. So what are the advantages?

Carp are incredibly aware of tackle, and particularly line. Lines strung out across swims from two or three rods, running over gravel bars or across weedbeds are not difficult for carp to see, often reducing your chances of action. Hiding your line, whether using lead core leaders, back leads or blobs of tungsten putty behind the rig have long since been standard practice for experienced carpers.

Using fluorocarbon main line allows you to conceal all of your line better than ever thanks to its physical properties. A very dense sinking line, it more readily follows the contours of the lake bed between rod tip and hook bait, ensuring your line is concealed and

laid more discreetly along the bottom, especially around the hook bait. So heavy is fluorocarbon main line that after casting light bobbins will slowly creep tight up to the rod blank as it sinks and settles to take up the contours of the lake bed beneath it.

A further advantage of fluorocarbon not often considered is that due to its increased weight and sinking properties it improves hooking.

Fluorocarbon lying along the lake bed for much of its length significantly adds to the resistance felt at the rig end when a carp tightens a hook length to the lead.

Until the launch of Fox Illusion fluorocarbon hasn't been widely available of sufficient quality or on big enough spools to use as a reel line, most fluorocarbons characterised by poor knot strengths lower than marked on the spools, high diameters and excessive memory making them impossible to cast and fish with effectively.

"Carp are incredibly aware of tackle, and particularly line"

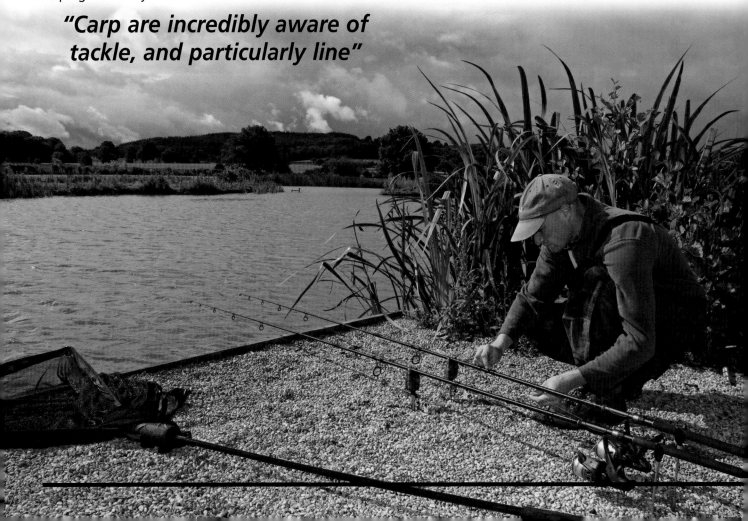

Illusion offers genuine knot strength, low diameters, high abrasion resistance and is supple for easy casting even at longer ranges.

Widely adopted both by carpers and specialists, Illusion fluorocarbon has had such an impact that thousands of anglers who have switched to it on the reels are unwilling to spool up with monofilament again.

TOP TIP

Because Illusion fluorocarbon sinks along its length it can become dirtied by contact with the lake bed. A dirty fluorocarbon does not have the same invisibility as a clean line. Periodically when retrieving run your Illusion through a cloth to remove any dirt on the surface of the line.

"Fluorocarbon has a light refractive index very close to that of water which makes it virtually invisible when submerged"

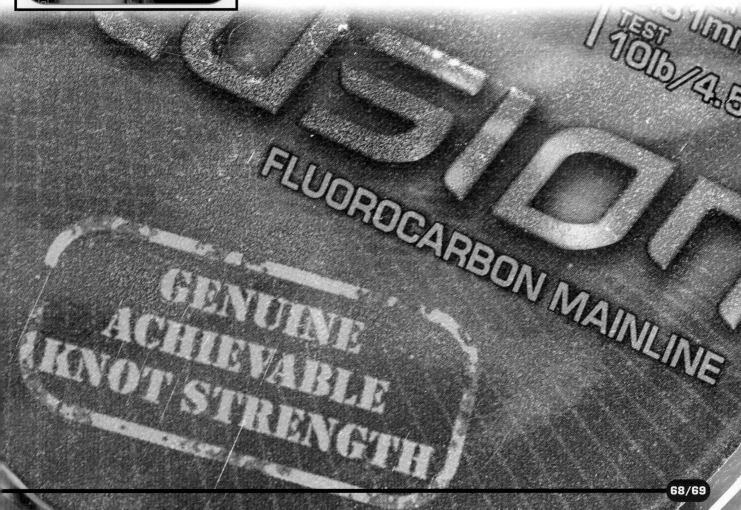

MONOFILAMENT

THE go anywhere carp line, there is very little that you can't do with a quality monofilament on the reels. Supple, easy casting and offering a versatile blend of knot strength and high abrasion resistance, if limited to one line for all your carp angling monofilament would get the vote.

Relative to braided lines and fluorocarbon, monofilament is the cheapest of the lines. The standard of monofilaments on offer today has also improved dramatically,

ensuring tremendous performance even from less costly lines.

Being so versatile and user friendly, and cheap enough to replace every few sessions if necessary it's no wonder mono still dominates the carp line market.

In the excitement over new specialist lines it is easy to forget just how reliable mono has been as a big fish reel line for decade after decade.

For example mono far outperforms braided Dyneema lines for abrasion resistance when the going gets tough despite the perception being that braids are the strongest line choice for demanding fishing situations.

Like a faithful dog, mono reliably does exactly what you ask of it time and time again without any fuss, it just performs and keeps performing.

A QUICK GUIDE TO MONOFILAMENT

A 12 lb mono makes a perfect all-purpose carp line, casting leads to around 3 oz up to 100 yards without a leader, or lighter leads and small cobweb PVA bags.

Highly abrasion resistant lines like Barbuster protect against losses from sharp gravel bars, line chafing through weed or touching branches and other submerged snags. The thicker a line the greater its abrasion resistance, making 15 lb monos ideal.

For larger solid style PVA bags and Method feeders the increased breaking strain and resilience of 15 lb mono is a more responsible choice to reduce the risk of snap-offs and tackle loss.

Fox Soft Steel Camo uses alternating sections of different subdued camouflage colours to help break its outline up underwater, disguising your tackle from wary carp.

"If limited to one line for all your carp angling monofilament would get the vote"

BRAIDS

A MUCH more specialist line choice, the carp world is split over the use of braided lines on the reel. Some love them, some loathe them, but they undoubtedly have a place in our armoury and at times help us catch extra fish.

Braided lines are manufactured from high performance polyethylene fibres which have virtually zero stretch. Braid's lack of stretch is its key characteristic. The effect on bite indication is remarkable, any movement of the line will be registered almost like for like at the bobbin and buzzer, and without the typical 10-15 per cent stretch of most monofilament there is no 'dampening' of any movement of the line. Using braid for the first time can be almost unnerving. Every movement is exaggerated and amplified - even line bites can smash a bobbin into the rod rather than creeping bobbins slowly up to the top.

Fast takes on mono can be exciting but using braided lines it can be a worrying prospect picking up a rod when a spool is spinning so quickly and a rod kicking in the rests so savagely.

Virtually zero stretch also makes playing carp a completely different proposition than when using mono. With no shock absorbing qualities in the braided line every movement a carp makes is directly transmitted to the rod. It can be a savage experience, and for every angler who loves the thrill and excitement braid introduces to the fight, there will be another angler who finds the direct contact unnerving and prefers to play carp on mono or fluorocarbon whose controlled stretch acts as a shock absorber to a carp's sudden twists, turns and head shakes.

The improved indication of braided lines is a huge plus, especially when tackling very rig-shy fish that are repeatedly picking up and ejecting rigs. With every movement of a hook length and lead accurately relayed to your buzzers the sensitivity of a braided line can help build a better picture of what is happening in a swim. There are numbers of anglers who routinely switch their reel lines to braid for the colder months when carp's feeding behaviour and movements are much less bold because of low water temperatures. Braid's sensitivity helps magnify the smallest movements, which can lead to more carp on the bank when 'takes' are only delicate pulls or a tightening of the line.

Braids also make excellent reel lines for long range fishing thanks to their ultra low diameter. Fox's 25 lb Submerge braid has a similar diameter to 8 lb mono allowing effortless long casting and adding yards to your casting range.

FLOATERS OR SINKERS?

DYNEEMA, the material that braids are manufactured from, is naturally buoyant. The majority of braided lines are therefore also buoyant, bringing problems with lines picking up weed and floating debris, suffering repeated false indications from wind or undertow and sitting high in the water where they are easily visible to carp.

Floating braids have their uses, specifically for spodding, but Fox only supply sinking braids for use as main lines, recognising the value of a line that quickly cuts through the surface film of water, sits low in the water and follows exactly the contours of the lake bed towards the end tackle for effective line concealment.

Many sinking braids have very loose weaves allowing water to penetrate the fibres and sink them, or use polyester to add weight to overcome the buoyancy of the Dyneema. Both result in braids with high diameters that cast badly. Using the latest woven fibre technology has resulted in Submerge Plus - a fast sinking braid that retains a tremendously fine diameter for exceptional casting performance.

Braided reel lines under tension can damage carp and lift scales during the fight. Always use a three foot (100cm) lead core leader or length of anti-tangle tube for safety.

25-35 foot mono or fluorocarbon leaders with braided main lines add a length of shock absorbing line to reduce the chances of hook pulls under the rod tip and before netting.

If using braided reel lines for long range fishing always tighten a reel's clutch before casting and use a finger stall to prevent the braid cutting into your index finger.

Splashing your reel spools with lake water before casting reduces the likelihood of wind knots, which are difficult to unpick and mostly result in you having to strip expensive braid off and bin it.

SPOOLING UP REELS: Monofilament and Fluorocarbon.

CORRECT spooling up prevents loading new line with unnecessary twist. Twisted lines are difficult to fish with, cast badly and often cause wrap rounds on rod rings that lead to snaps off and tackle loss. Often the line is blamed but the fault lies with the angler for failing to load it correctly on the reels. Monofilament and fluorocarbon are both loaded the same way.

1. Fill a bucket with 7-10cm of hot water straight out of the tap - typically 60 degrees Centigrade. Leave the spool of line to be loaded to soak in the hot water for a few minutes. This softens and lubricates the line.

2. Stand the spool upright in the bucket so the coils of line are peeling off anti-clockwise. It helps with some spools to pierce labels to prevent air being trapped inside the drum of the spool.

3. Tie a grinner knot around your fingers with the end of the line, leaving you with a large loop. Slip the loop over the spool of the reel to be filled, tighten down and trim the tag end.

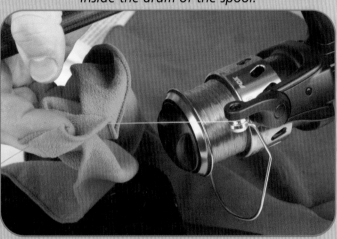

4. Close the bale arm and lightly trap the line inside a towel or cloth in front of the reel. Wind the line on under steady tension, checking the spool in the bucket remains in upright and doesn't flip over.

5. Keep loading until the spool is filled to within a few millimetres of the lip for optimum casting performance. Overfilled spools cause bird's nests on the cast which leads to snap offs and line loss.

6. Carry spare spools loaded with different breaking strains and types of lines. For most UK fishing spools of 12 lb (0.33mm) Illusion and either 12 or 15 lb Warrior, Barbuster or Soft Steel will cover almost any situation.

LOADING BRAID Braided lines do not accommodate or suffer twist in the same way mono or fluorocarbon lines do, making spooling up with them and keeping them in good condition on the reel much easier.

All braids benefit from soaking overnight in water prior to spooling up

Load braid by putting a pencil through the centre of the spool and winding it under tension on to the reel through a cloth or towel.

Don't load braid right to the lip like you would mono. A 2mm gap below the spool lip helps prevent wind knots and bird's nests.

LOADING TO THE LIP EVERY TIME

EVER got halfway through re-spooling a reel only to run out of line? Most lines are supplied on bulk spools and the majority of carp reels boast generous line capacity, meaning they can swallow hundreds of yards of quality line if you fill them top to bottom. Guessing how well your line will fill a spool is a waste of time. Get it wrong and you'll only end up having to take the line off again which can be messy and costly. Reels need to be correctly filled for smooth casting and optimum clutch operation, without constantly paying for line you never see or use. Here's how...

For braided lines, fluorocarbons or monos that are supplied on one shot spools that might not necessarily accurately fill your reel spool there's a simple method for ensuring you load lines right to the lip of the spool every time instead of guessing and coming up short or overfilling.

1. You'll need a reel with two empty spools. Tie a loop with a grinner knot and tighten it down on to one spool.

2. Now load the line on to the reel until it runs out. In most instances you will still have a significantly under filled spool.

3. Tie some cheap, high diameter mono like 15 lb Warrior to the line on the spool using a double grinner knot and trim the tag ends.

4. Now load the Warrior mono on to the reel over the top of your chosen line until it is filled flush to the lip of the spool.

5. Remove the filled spool from the reel and replace it with the empty one. Take the end of the Warrior mono and tie it to the empty spool.

6. Now wind all of the contents of the filled spool back on to the empty one, in effect reversing them so your chosen line is perfectly backed up with mono and sits flush to the lip of the spool.

SPOOL REDUCERS

Fox Stratos reels are supplied with spool reducing collars, dropping their capacity for UK fishing. Capacities are clearly marked on the spools for different diameter main lines allowing you to judge exactly how many reels you can fill from a bulk spool.

LINE MARKING

Illusion fluorocarbon is supplied on 300 metre spools, but features a line marking sticker at 150 yards, allowing you to accurately split the spool between two reels. Because fluorocarbon isn't a distance casting line 150 yards is adequate for most carp fishing situations.

CHAPTER 5

SPODDING

SPODDING

CARP bait comes in a huge variety of shapes and sizes, from hemp to maggots, corn and boilies. Although boilies can be fed at medium to long range with powerful catapults and throwing sticks, a huge number of successful baits are lightweight or irregularly shaped making them difficult to catapult anything other than short distances.

Remote boats are expensive and beyond the pocket of many carpers and baiting from rowing boats is banned on most UK venues, leaving one key method for introducing feed - spodding.

Devised back in the early 80s spods or bait rockets are the most effective way to accurately feed small baits long distances. Filled with any combination of baits, from grains of hemp to the tiniest micro pellets spods are simply cast to the required area.

A buoyant nose cone ensures they flip over after hitting the water and simply drop your feed in a tight area below the rocket.

The latest computer designed rockets are aerodynamic and incredibly stable in flight, coupled with powerful spod rods they allow us to be able to consistently bait with the tiniest of feeds within feet of a target even at very long ranges - subject to your casting accuracy. A good caster with balanced tackle can launch well designed spods up to 150 yards, beyond the ranges many can effectively cast baited rigs.

Test a reel before you buy it, if mono comes out of the clip with any marking or damage to it, avoid the reel. All Fox reels have cushioned spool clips for safe retention of line and accurate casting whether with spods or end tackles.

SPOD RODS

LARGE spods are far heavier than any leads we will ever cast. Spod rods have to be powerful to take the repeated strain of launching loads that may reach 6-8 oz. The Warrior Spod retails at around £60 but features a crisp, progressive action that effortlessly powers heavy rockets up to 120 yards and beyond if your casting technique allows. It handles loads to 8 oz and features triple legged Fox Slik guides perfectly positioned to smoothly cone the line flow from a big pit reel for longer casting. A 16mm tip ring allows easy passage of leader knots even when fouled with weed or debris and the non-slip coated handle and shrink tube butt retain grip even when covered in liquids from filling rockets with wet spod mixes.

WARRIOR SPOD - 12' 5.50lb

The **Horizon SFD Spod** uses advanced blank construction and low profile Titanium lightweight ringing from a 48mm butt to a 16mm tip for extreme casting performance. At 4.25 lb test curve spods in excess of 4 oz compress the blank most effectively. The Horizon SFD Spod is the choice for longer range work and has cast a fully loaded TB1 spod in excess of 140 yards.

"The Fox Stratos 12000 MAG has unrivalled line lay - ideal for extreme range casting with end tackles and spods"

SPOD REELS

FOR heavier spods and baiting at longer ranges big pit reels have become standard issue on spod rods.

The adoption of larger spooled big pit reels is not because they cast further than smaller spooled reels. With fine braid or mono reel lines there is little appreciable difference in casting potential of big pit reels versus smaller models.

The key advantage is simply that when using a big pit model each turn of the handle retrieves more line than using a smaller spooled model, making shorter work of repeated long retrieves.

As well as good line lay it's essential that a spod reel has a line friendly spool clip to allow main line to be clipped and rockets to be repeatedly landed in exactly the right area.

SPOD LINES
MAIN LINE

SPODDING puts heavy demands on a reel line, with repeated casting and retrieving in all conditions and at all ranges. Braided reel lines are widely accepted as the most effective choice. Their low diameter allows rockets to be cast in excess of 120 yards with ease, minimising the effect of crosswinds on accuracy. Naturally buoyant, braid stays on the surface after a spod has touched down, allowing it to be effortlessly picked up from the surface film by lifting the rod tip, making retrieval quicker and easier. Braid also stores much less twist than mono from repeated casting and retrieving, leading to far fewer problems with wind knots and the reel line grabbing the butt ring on the cast - both of which often cause crack offs and lost rockets.

Fox Spod Braid uses ultra strong bonded Dyneema filaments and is incredibly tough and hard wearing. Breaking at over 30 lb it can be used without a shock leader to cast small and medium rockets. Its fluoro yellow finish ensures it is visible in all conditions, preventing tangles and crossovers when positioning baited rigs around the spodded area.

The only drawback of braid is its higher price than mono, but because braid does not degrade in ultra violet light (sunshine) like mono and much less readily suffers wind knots after the initial expense it often lasts several seasons on a reel with no loss in performance or breaking strain.

If you are on a tight budget you can use 8-10 lb mono for a spod reel line instead of braid. But for regular spodding it might be a false economy, needing to be replaced every few sessions to prevent twisting, weakening and crack offs. Also beware that the small amount you save spooling up with light mono on a spod reel you can easily lose and more if you crack several spods off through not looking after and replacing mono regularly.

TYING A SHOCK LEADER KNOT

A RELIABLE join between your light reel line and shock leader is essential. Many anglers lack confidence tying leader knots but if you can tie strong, consistent knots to swivels and hooks you should achieve the same reliability when tying line to line. The double grinner knot or Mahin knot are both recommended when joining heavy and light nylon or heavy nylon to fine braid.

Fox Soft Steel Tapered Leaders offer a high breaking strain to absorb the power of casting heavy spods, tapering into a finer mono to reduce resistance in flight and gain extra distance. The finer diameter also makes knots between reel line and leader less bulky, flying through the rings with minimum effort even when casting extreme range. Tapered Leaders are 12 metres long and available in two strains 12-35 lb and 15-45 lb. Use the heaviest Tapered Leaders when casting TB1 spods, the lighter version for TB2 versions with fine braided reel lines.

Braided shock leaders like Fox Armadillo help compress rods quicker because of their lack of stretch and are useful for long and extreme range spodding. Braided leaders can also be tied with the double grinner knot detailed here.

TYING A SHOCK LEADER KNOT

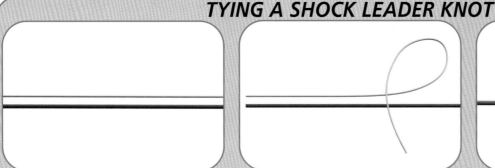

1. The finer end of the Tapered Leader comes off the spool first for convenience. Run the last 12-15cm of your reel line parallel to the finer end of the Tapered Leader.

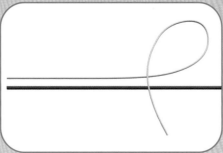

2. Grip the tag end of the reel line and turn it back on itself anti-clockwise. Trap it between finger and thumb so you have a large loop with 5-7cm of line protruding downwards.

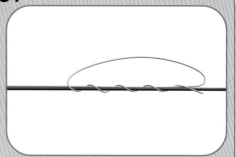

3. Maintain your grip with finger and thumb, and with the other hand pass the tag end down and around the leader and then through the loop towards you.

4. Repeat this five times, effectively whipping the loop to the shock leader that is lying parallel to it.

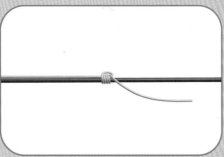

5. Moisten the loop with saliva to lubricate it and gently pull the tag end to tighten it down. As the knot tightens and forms a distinctive figure of eight push the base of the knot upwards with finger and thumb as you pull the tag end to bed it right down.

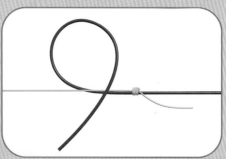

6. Gripping the knot between finger and thumb take the tag end of the Tapered Leader and turn it back on itself clockwise to form a loop running parallel to the main line.

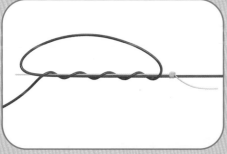

7. Gripping the loop between finger and thumb pass the tag end of the Leader around the reel line and back through the loop five times.

8. Tighten down as before. The knot should bed down a few inches away from the first knot.

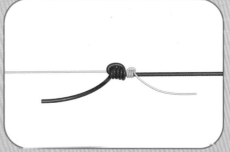

9. Cover both knot barrels with saliva then steadily pull the leader and the reel line. Both knots will be pulled together to form a neat barrel with two long tag ends.

"If you can tie strong, consistent knots to swivels and hooks you can achieve the same reliability tying line to line"

10. Trim the tag ends neatly at around 2mm for a neat, secure shock leader knot that will take the strain of casting heavy spods or leads.

WHICH SPOD?

SPODS can come in all shapes and sizes. Traditionally rockets of different designs needed to be carried for baiting at different ranges and with different feeds. The Fox TB range of spods overcomes the need for carrying different spods by using a range of inserts to alter their suitability with different baits. All the inserts clip and slide in and out easily with finger pressure.

TB spods without inserts can be used for all normal dry or dampened bait mixes. Adding the half cylinder insert improves performance with wet, sticky particle mixes. Blanking the base of the chamber prevents attractive liquids being lost from the mix after loading that are much more beneficial suspended in the water around your marker float pulling carp to the target area than dropping on your head or in your swim before the spod is cast.

The full length blanking insert allows you to fill a spod completely with water. Casting to a marker float or visible feature you can range find without spreading spod fulls of feed away from your baited area, then you can clip the main line at the reel to ensure consistent baiting (see Accuracy, pg 96).

Full length inserts also allow us to spod combinations of liquids rather than solid feeds. It's an increasingly popular tactic when fishing zig rigs mid-water or higher or in the winter when carp need maximum stimulation to feed but increasing solid food items in the swim is counter productive.

Combinations of boilie dips, evaporated milk, tiger nut syrup and liquidised sweetcorn thinned with lake water will produce attractive long lasting taste and smell clouds in the water.

CAPACITIES

KNOWING the capacity of your spod and its weight fully loaded helps improve safety, allowing us to use correct leaders and balanced rod, reel and main line for easier baiting.

SPOD	TB1	TB2	TB3
EMPTY	2.25oz	1oz	1.25oz
FILLED WITH PELLET/HEMP	6.9oz	3oz	4.25oz
BAIT PAYLOAD	4.65oz	2oz	3oz

STUBBY SPODS

SPODDING doesn't always need to involve long casting and spare rods and reels rigged up with huge capacity rockets. The TB2 Stubby Spod is purpose designed for feeding smaller quantities of bait. Although it can be cast long distances it is best used as a short to medium range tool where its accuracy allows tiny handfuls of free offerings to be added to a swim with much less disturbance than when using bigger TB1 and TB3 models.

Weighing only 3 oz when fully loaded with hemp and pellet they are too light to compress high test curve spod rods and are comfortably and more accurately cast using standard carp rods of 2.5 to 3 lb test curve and 12-15 lb mono reel lines straight through without a shock leader.

Carrying a couple of TB2 Stubby Spods gives you the flexibility to quickly and quietly introduce small baits like hemp and micro pellets at short to medium range with the minimum of disturbance and without having to carry a spod rod and reel outfit with you.

SAFETY

REPEATEDLY casting any heavy projectile brings with it potential dangers, both to you and your tackle. Safety checks and good practice help minimise the dangers.

FINGER PROTECTION

Because of the pressure from a heavy loaded spod transmitted through the line as the rod is wound up on the cast it's easy to damage the tip of your index finger that grips the line before releasing the cast. A leather finger stall from the local chemist or a leather golf glove protects your finger even during heavy baiting sessions.

CHECK THE CLUTCH

Often we slacken clutches to store or re-assemble made up rods. Before spodding always ensure the clutch of your spod reel is screwed up tightly again. With the power generated when casting a heavy spod a slack clutch can slip, pulling the line across a finger tip and slicing through your skin. With braided leaders or braid fished straight through you could cut your finger to the bone.

LEADERS

Shock leaders can be left on spod rods between sessions but always check the knot and the rest of the leader for signs of damage before starting to bait up. A damaged leader is weakened which can lead to expensive and dangerous spod losses. Run your finger and thumb along it to check for nicks or abrasions.

WRAP AROUNDS

Before casting always check the line is running freely not snagged around the rod tip. Pull the line above the reel to check the leader runs smoothly through the rings to pull the spod cleanly up and down. It becomes second nature and prevents crack offs or smashed rods where strong line is wrapped around the top couple of inches of the rod.

PREVENTING SPOD SPILL

ONE of the most common complaints when spodding is that many rockets have a tendency to lose a percentage of their load during the early part of the cast, showering feed items between the rods and the area being fished. Introducing feed anywhere other than the intended target doesn't improve our chances of catching.

Spod spill is most common with lighter feeds such as small pellets and hemp, although even larger baits like boilies can be lost in flight. There are many factors that affect spill from the inertia of the feed in the rocket to how closely the bait or combination of bait sits together inside the spod to the movement of air behind the top of the chamber in flight and how much bait it has been filled with.

A simple tactic that reduces spod spill is to use the full length insert supplied with the Fox TB series of spods. Blanking the holes in the body of the spod prevents air pushing through the spod and dislodging feed so readily in the early stages of the cast and allows us to quickly dunk the spod under the rod tip and fill the chamber with water prior to casting. Water sat over the top of the feed adds weight over it which also prevents it falling out so readily.

For combinations of smaller baits like hemp, mixed particle and small pellets a better answer is to mix the spod mix in advance, allowing the juices from the hemp or particle to soak into and soften the pellets. After loading the dampened pellets, a gentle push with your thumb compresses the feed in the spod, stopping it from spilling on the cast but still allowing it to fall cleanly from the spod when water floods the chamber after touchdown. You'll see clearly if you continue to spill feed in flight. If so the bait needs to be slightly damper or compressed more firmly. As long as it is empty when retrieved you can be sure the feed is being dumped cleanly out of the spod in the target area.

TOP TIP

Ian Chillcott mixes a small quantity of pellet with water to soften it and then uses a small amount of this soft pellet as a plug in the top of the spod. Fill the spod two thirds full with bait of your choice, whether boilies, particle or dry pellet, press a small soft pellet plug in the top, then cast out. This ensures all your bait will land exactly where you want it to.

TO SPOD OR NOT?

SPODDING is a way of life on most popular carp waters. Popping a marker float up on a likely area and routinely spodding kilo after kilo of pellet, hemp or boilies is a feature of the start of a session for tens of thousands of carpers each week. Spodding is a tremendously effective method of accurately introducing feeds of all types and sizes, but is not always appropriate or beneficial.

WHEN TO SPOD

1. Longer sessions of 48 hours or more lend themselves to spodding bigger baited areas, allowing the carp to visit the area and become more confident. It's always a gamble but you have to weigh up the initial disturbance caused by the spod against the possibility of a multiple catch later in the session.

2. One or a couple of accurately cast spod loads around a hook bait can be incredibly successful on waters that see big spodded areas. Carp are used to finding odd patches of feed from miscast spods, and they are almost always safe to eat.

3. Unlike on more pressurised venues where the sound of a spod easily spooks carp, on busy, well stocked waters where multiple catches of carp are possible the sound of the spod is often associated with more food arriving in the swim. Topping up with a couple of fresh spods of bait can be enough to bring more action.

4. Spods aren't just for hemp, pellet and particle baits. Use them to introduce mini boilies and 'chops' or pellet shaped baits at any range.

5. Part filling spods and spreading the same quantity of bait more widely rather than concentrated in a few square feet around a marker float and hook bait can also pay dividends.

WHEN NOT TO SPOD

1. Don't automatically spod free offerings out at the start of a session. Always start with stringers, small PVA bags or even single hook baits, watching for signs of carp and seeing where they are most active. You can always decide to build a baited area later if conditions look good and you are in the right area.

2. When you have lots of carp in front of you, especially on smaller or busier waters don't cast spods or marker floats on top of their heads. By being more cautious and fishing bags, stringers or hook baits you might catch a few quickly rather than spooking them from in front of you.

3. Beware spodding becomes addictive. It is satisfying seeing a rocket land bang on a marker float time and time again. It's very easy to get carried away and introduce more bait than you intended.

4. Don't spod at times of the day or night that are productive for action like dawn and dusk. Try and feed a swim or top up at times when there is a reduced chance of action or fish activity is less pronounced.

MAXIMUM distance and improved accuracy is achieved by only two thirds filling a spod with feed. Loading a spod to the top of the chamber affects its stability in flight which reduces distance.

TOP TIP

WHEN spodding hemp, pellet and particle you encourage carp to hoover up small food items which can make them tricky to hook. Over hard bottoms with big baited areas shorten hook lengths down to 10-12cm to hook carp that are 'grazing'. Use bottom baits or balanced baits rather then pop-ups, and keep them small. The greater the quantity of feed in the swim the more productive baits are fished hard on the bottom.

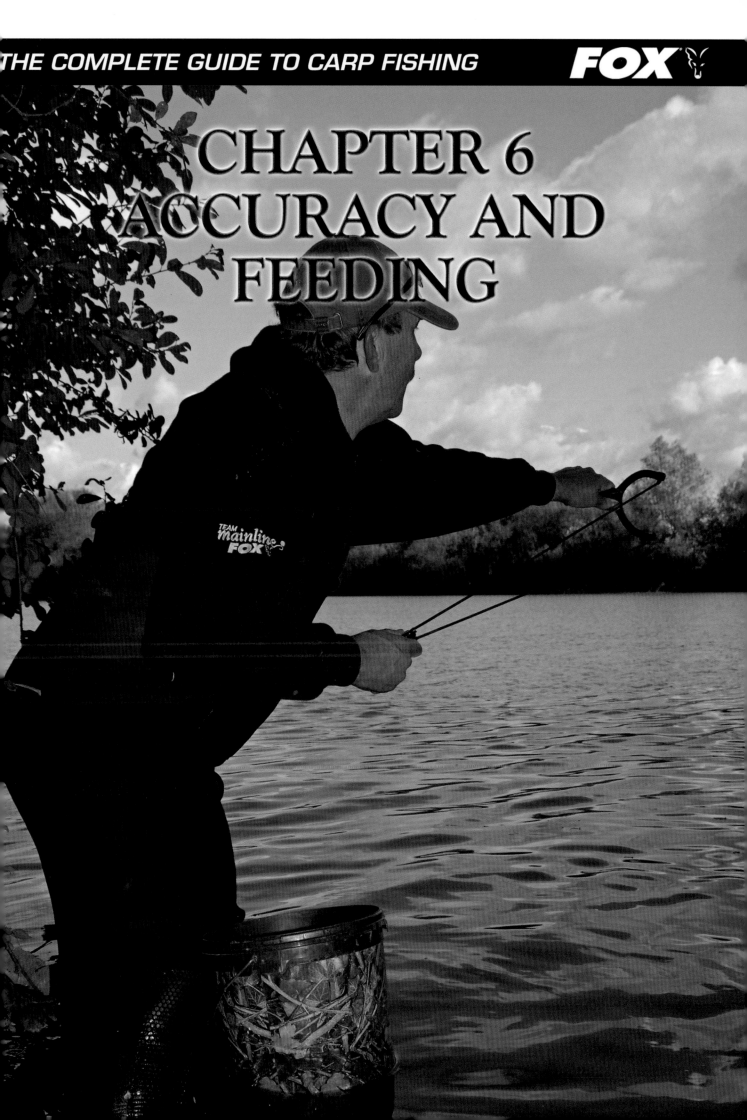

CHAPTER 6
ACCURACY AND
FEEDING

ACCURACY

THE ability to cast and bait accurately is fundamental to successful carp angling. Although carp have sufficiently keen senses to locate the smallest items of food anywhere in a lake, grouping free offerings tightly attracts carp to the hook bait and significantly improves our chances of catching.

Casting accuracy is crucial. A few yards away from the target area can see your rig at the bottom of a shelf surrounding an island margin rather than tight to the margin in shallower water where it will be more readily taken by patrolling carp. On gravel pits a few yards can make the difference between presenting hook baits on a productive bar or gravel feature and in foul smelling silt.

Weedy waters demand pinpoint accuracy to present baits in holes or strips of clean bottom between the underwater vegetation.
Any variation in distance or direction of a cast will often see tackle sat amongst weed stems and you not fishing effectively at all.

Whether trying to land tight to marker floats or more natural visual targets like islands, tree canopies or lilies casting baited rigs or loaded spods requires an identical technique, called clipping up. Once mastered it allows you to consistently cast hook baits and feed in exactly the same place irrespective of the time of day or night or prevailing weather conditions.

CLIPPING UP

1. Make sure your marker float is positioned exactly where you want to fish with the right colour tip to make it highly visible as a casting target. Cock it correctly to reduce the dangers of fouling the marker rod with an end tackle.

2. Look along the skyline for markers such as telegraph poles, dips or changes in the shape of the tree line or buildings. You need to find a direction marker that coincides with the direction of your marker float and baited area. For day sessions you can use visual targets like fence posts, other swims and gates but for night sessions your sight reference needs to be obvious - hence using the skyline.

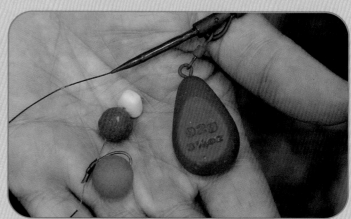

3. If nothing notable on the skyline corresponds with the direction of your marker float walk up and down the bank and look from places other than directly behind the rods in order to 'move' an obvious marker to coincide with the required direction. Push a tent peg in or position a stone to ensure you don't forget where you need to cast from.

4. On the rod to be cast to the marker you'll need either an end tackle tied up and with no hook length attached, or push a pop-up over the point of your hook to prevent any chance of the hook point being blunted through hitting bottom and being retrieved several times.

5. Cast at the marker float from the position you have chosen in the swim that gives you an obvious direction marker on the skyline as well. Remember, the float won't be there when you want to recast.

6. As the lead is dropping towards the water feather the line by pushing your index finger towards the spool and slowing the line as it leaves the reel. When the lead hits the water stop the line completely by pushing the tip of your index finger hard down on to up spool.

7. Did the lead land close enough to the marker float? Always aim to land the rig within a couple of feet of the marker, one side or the other. If the lead landed too short, too long or too far to the side of the float reel in and cast again.

8. When the lead lands tight to the float, slip the reel line into the casting clip on the spool. Be careful not to allow any more line to peel off the spool from under your finger before it's safely clipped. Close the bail arm.

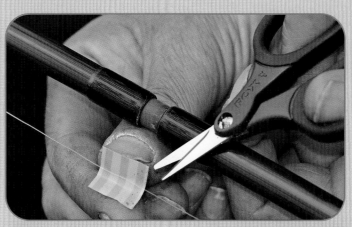

9. Put the rod either on the rests or on the floor and cut a 1.5-2cm strip of electrical tape. Fold the tape over the line directly underneath the middle spigot of the rod. Squeeze it hard so it sticks firmly both to the line and to itself and then trim it to around 2-3mm wide.

10. Leaving the line in the spool clip reel in and bait your hook length and attach your PVA bag ready for casting out. Cast towards the marker and as long as you cast hard enough the line will be pulled off the reel until it hits the spool clip, stopping the rig and dropping it right next to the float.

11. You must remove the line from the spool clip before setting your Hanger or Swinger and bite alarm. When you get a take the carp will need to pull line from the reel using the free spool. You could have a rod pulled off the rests if you leave the line in the spool clip.

12. After catching a carp cast back out away from your baited area - being careful of other anglers and lines - until you see or hear the electrical tape marker on the line fly through the rings. Wind back until the tape is under the middle spigot and slip the line into the spool clip at the reel.

13. Check your hook, rebait your rig and add a PVA bag if required. Standing in the same position as before cast towards your chosen skyline marker. As long as the lead lands in the right direction and the line is pulled tight to the clip on the spool when it lands your hook bait will have dropped accurately over the feed again.

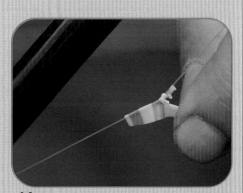

14. Tape markers can be pulled off the line between finger and thumb at the end of each session or if you change the position of a rod. If you have to strip off any line from above your end tackle through damage measure how much is removed and position a new marker the same distance further back up the line to compensate.

ACCURATE SPODDING

LANDING spods consistently in the same place to keep a baited area tight uses exactly the same method of clipping up.

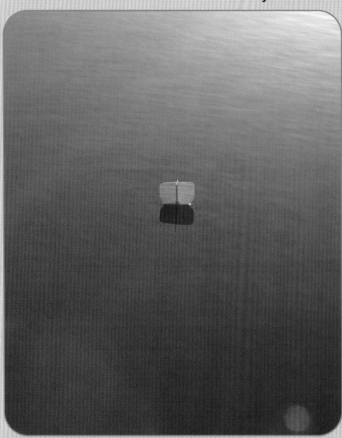

1. After your marker float is in place find a position in the swim or along the bank that gives you an obvious skyline direction marker to coincide with the position of the float.

2. Slip the full cylinder insert into one of the Fox TB spods and dunk it under the rod tip to fill it full of water as casting weight. This allows you to cast as many times as required to find the correct range without spreading unwanted bait around the swim.

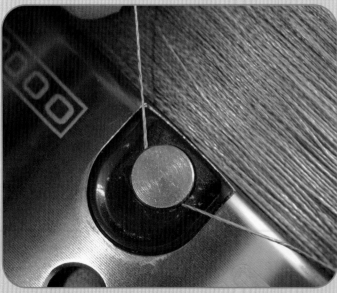

3. Cast the spod towards the float until it lands accurately and then clip the braid in the spool clip and mark the line under the middle spigot with an electrical tape marker as detailed in steps 8 and 9 in the previous pages.

4. The braid stays in the clip for as long as the session duration. As long as you cast hard enough to pull the line off the reel to hit the clip the spod will drop on a sixpence on the baited area every time it's cast in the direction of your skyline marker.

SEMI-PERMANENT DISTANCE MARKERS

IT only takes a mishap with a marker rod, cracking off a spod or tangling lines whilst playing carp to lose the position of an electrical tape marker for accurate baiting or casting. If you've spent a lot of time locating and feeding small hotspots it's frustrating to be unable to find the area again with confidence. Using semi-permanent markers along the bank measures out the distance to clip up to drop over your baited area.

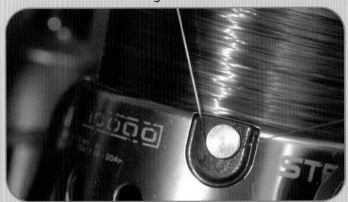

1. After clipping up at the correct distance for your marker float and baited area wind the end tackle back in from the baited area.

2. Place the end tackle on the bank next to a bivvy peg behind your bivvy or an obvious marker like a fence or gate post.

3. Open the bale arm and walk back along the bank, keeping the line tight to the lead on the floor with finger pressure being careful not to move it.

4. When you've hit the spool clip, ensure the line is straight back to your end tackle and bankside marker and lie the rod and reel on the floor. Push another peg or a stick in next to the reel.

5. If you lose line and need to reposition marker tape place your rig by the marker behind the bivvy, walk the rod open bale arm along the bank and at the second bank side marker clip the line into the spool clip and stick on a new tape marker under the spigot.

CREEPING UP TO CANOPIES

WHEN positioning rigs tight to overhanging canopies, lily beds or snags like fallen trees there's a risk of tackle loss if you overcast whilst trying to find the correct range to clip up. Even the most accomplished caster will be unlikely to land a rig inches from the target first time, and if you overshoot you can lose tackle in trees which can be a danger to both anglers and yourself.

The answer is to deliberately drop your first couple of casts short, and then gradually increase the amount of line that needs to be pulled from the reel to hit the clip until the rig lands perfectly.

1. The rig is cast deliberately short of the required target area, the finger trapping the line on the spool as the lead hits the water.

2. Keeping your finger on the spool estimate how far short of the target area the cast landed - in this case a rod length.

3. Pull slightly less than a rod length of line from the reel and clip it at the spool clip. Now retrieve the end tackle.

4. Cast again from the same position in the swim and see where the rig lands. If it appears six feet short, take the line from the spool clip, pull another four feet from the reel and then slip it into the clip again and retrieve the end tackle.

5. Being cautious and gradually lengthening the distance the lead can travel before being stopped by the spool clip allows you to 'creep' up each time until the line is clipped perfectly to drop the rig in within inches of the tree line or snag.

6. Punch the cast (1) so it travels hard and low rather than lobbing it high. Punching helps land rigs tight to your chosen feature. Even small changes in trajectory of 'lobbed' casts (2) can see you land in the trees even though you're clipped up.

TARGET AREA
X

X
INITIAL CAST

INITIAL CAST 12ft
SHORT OF TARGET X

SUBSEQUENT ATTEMPTS 'CREEP'
CLOSER TO TARGET AS A FEW FEET
OF LINE IS PULLED FROM THE REEL
AND RE-CLIPPED BETWEEN CASTS

THROWING STICKS

PURPOSE designed for loose feeding boilies beyond catapult range throwing sticks allow large, hard baits to be launched over 100 yards.

With the increase in use of smaller feeds like pellet and hemp throwing sticks have become less popular, spods being the first choice baiting tool for most carpers beyond catapult range. But sticks do have important tactical advantages.

Bait can be introduced to top up a swim with very little disturbance, boilies being skipped along the surface and entering with barely a noise, which can prevent spooking feeding carp. In contrast spods are a tremendously noisy, invasive method of baiting.

Spods score because they allow us to bait as accurately as we can cast, and most carpers can cast more accurately than they can use a throwing stick. Good technique and practice can see sticks drop baits in tight areas but their downfall is that any variation or flaw in technique sees baits scattered more widely in a swim. But once mastered they are an easy way to bait, with no elastics or pouches to replace or heavy extra rods and reels to carry.

Wider baiting can itself be advantageous, especially when feeding larger boilies. With such mainstream use of spods to bait tight areas, scattering boilies with a stick has become a very successful method on many hard fished venues. Carp find one bait at a time which is much less alarming, and encouraging carp to move and search for another bait can lead to easier hooking than when carp are feeding on small items in a very tightly baited area.

STRAIGHT OR CURVED?

STICKS come in two distinct designs, curved and straight. Straight sticks are easiest to master, requiring a simple straight flick forwards to punch baits at the target area in a swim. At shorter to medium range they are superbly accurate. Using curved sticks accurately is more difficult. They generate more spin on a bait, sending them much greater distances but any deviation in the swing forwards in the stick can send baits significantly off target.

Available to fit boilies up to 18, 24 and 30mm Fox Rangemaster curved sticks are CAD designed for maximum velocity and distance. Ultra light construction allows heavy baiting without fatigue and the non-slip rubberised handle provides a solid grip even with wet hands.

BOILIES need to be perfectly round to fly straight from a throwing stick, so check you are using well rolled, round baits. Because they are dried

for longer shelf-life baits are harder and fly effortlessly out of a stick. Softer frozen ready-mades can split as they exit the stick and in flight. Periodically wetting the inside of the stick by dunking it in the margins and then shaking the water out helps. Alternatively, air dry frozen ready-mades for a few days before your session. They become harder and less likely to split but being lighter will not travel as far.

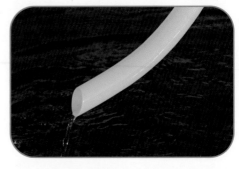

BAIT DROPPERS

ALTHOUGH designed for getting bait down to the bottom in flowing water for barbel and chub, Fox Bait Droppers have applications for big carp. Bait cages with a trap door mechanism, droppers are cast or lowered into a swim and empty their contents when the weighted base hits bottom, triggering the retaining catch and allowing bait to spill out.

Tied to a spare rod they allow feed to be tightly grouped even in deep water when margin fishing, particularly when stalking around overhanging trees and snag bushes. Available in different sizes droppers also allow small, light baits like hemp, pellets and maggots to be delivered direct to the lake bed where small fish populations can be problematical.

With straight sticks stand with your feet shoulder width apart and the stick upright at head height. Keeping it pointing at the desired target and with a short backswing punch the stick forwards swiftly, extending your arm.

Curved sticks demand more of a swing. Hold them at head height, then bring them back and push forwards and extend the arm with more of a casting motion.

FOX

CATAPULTS

AT shorter ranges there is still nothing to beat a catapult for quick, accurate introduction of free offerings. With different design pouches and varying strength elastics you can find a catapult to feed any carp bait. Using the right pouch improves accuracy and bait grouping. As a rule the smaller the pouch the fewer baits it holds and the further it is intended to fire them.

AVOIDING KNUCKLE RAP

IT'S PAINFUL when a pouch or elastics rap you on the knuckles when baiting. Although rapped knuckles are largely preventable with good technique, it catches even the most experienced carpers out. The Fox Power Guard catapult series use a patented knuckle defender that protects the hand during use. With one piece moulded pouches to prevent weak spots, ergonomic handles to suit left and right-handers and carefully chosen latex, Power Guards group baits with pinpoint accuracy without any discomfort.

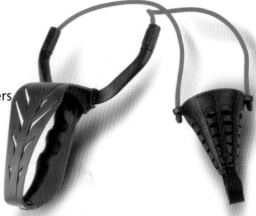

SPARES

REPLACEMENT elastics and pouches are available for all Fox catapults. Spares kits for the carp catapult range consist of both pouch and elastic, ensuring if there is a breakage you have the kit required for a repair. Look for wear to elastic where it exits or joins the frame.

PARTICLE POUCHES are the biggest, holding hemp, pellets and corn for tight grouping of small baits at short range.

MULTI POUCHES are all-rounders, able to hold multiple smaller boilies or larger pellets, effective at up to 50 yards but also suitable for shorter ranges with particles.

METHOD POUCHES are moulded to support balls of groundbait, preventing them being damaged or distorted as the elastic is pulled back.

BOILIE POUCHES are for single, larger boilies only. Twinned with strong elastic hard baits can be catapulted up to 90-100 yards.

TOP TIP

FOR improved accuracy and bait grouping cup the loaded catapult pouch in your hand rather than holding the finger pull at the base of the pouch. Keep your right arm locked rather than bent when drawing the elastic back.

FEEDING OVER FOAM

FOX High Riser Foam is a superb aid for accurate feeding at shorter ranges. These white foam nuggets can be hooked or wetted and squeezed on to hooks before casting. Dependent upon water temperature they dissolve away from the hook within 10-30 seconds and float to the surface where the white foam makes an easily spotted visual marker for feeding free offerings around the hook bait without needing a marker float. It's a great dodge when wanting to sprinkle a pouchful or two of larger pellets or boilies around a hook bait. It will take some experience to determine how far you will be able to accurately catapult different sized free offerings, but is a quick, easy and accurate way to bait around a rig without needing marker floats and spods for shorter range rods.

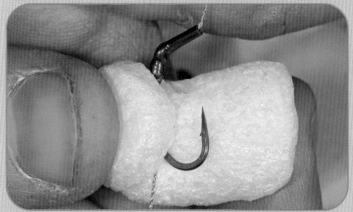

1. After nicking on a cobweb PVA bag lick a nugget of High Riser and squeeze it around the shank of the hook and the hair.

2. Load the pouch of a catapult with marine pellets or boilies and leave it on the floor in the swim by your feet. Prop it on a bait bag so the contents don't spill out while you are casting.

3. Cast out, and after the rig has hit the water put the rod carefully on the floor in the swim beside you and pick up the catapult.

4. Keep watching the surface of the water where the rig landed. After a few seconds you'll see the white nugget of High Riser Foam pop to the surface directly over the rig.

5. Keeping your eyes on the foam as a target marker catapult the pouchful of free offerings around the foam. If you want to introduce more bait there'll be time to reload the pouch and use the rings from the first helping of bait hitting the water to guide you even if the foam has drifted away.

6. Large pouches such as on the medium range multi pouch Fox catapult will fire multiple baits and group them most efficiently. Cup the pouch in the whole of your hand.

CHAPTER 7
THE METHOD

THE METHOD

EXPLOITING a carp's natural greed the Method is a tremendous tactic for carp big and small. Originally developed on commercial style match venues the principle of the Method is to introduce a large, compact ball of bait firmly moulded around a lead or feeder to develop aggressive, competitive feeding.

A ball of bait the size of a tangerine or even a small orange is a huge piece of food compared to any that a carp normally finds, and fish instinctively attack it. Because the bait is moulded stiffly around the feeder carp have to work hard, nosing, rolling and shaking the ball of bait to break food away from it. With numbers of carp present in a swim the added competition between fish leads to frenzied feeding.

Using the Method you can quickly tell if there are carp in your swim. Every time a carp noses or attacks a loaded Method feeder the rod top will shake or there will be a few bleeps at the buzzer and your indicator will repeatedly pull up and down as the groundbait ball is knocked around on the lake bed. It is normally only a matter of time before a carp picks up the hook bait and you receive a proper reel spinning take.

As effective as it is the Method is not a delicate way of catching carp, many imagining the sound of a loaded feeder hitting the water to be enough to spook any pressured carp. It's not a margin tactic and is perhaps not suitable for some small, very heavily fished venues, producing best when there are numbers of carp to fish for. But there are few carp waters that will not respond to feeder tactics. The deep splosh made by a loaded feeder bothers carp much less than you may think. It resembles noises made by other rolling and crashing carp much more than the distinctive crash of heavy lead rigs, and sometimes even prompts other carp nearby to roll shortly after the feeder lands.

In recent seasons it's been shown that the Method can be hugely successful with big carp, with plenty of 30s, 40s and even 50s reported on the tactic. Hugely versatile the Method makes a great carp trap whether used in weed, over silt or on hard bottoms like gravel. But it's an active tactic and demands time mixing groundbait correctly, and accuracy when casting, recasting and feeding. Because of this it remains one of the most under used modern carp tactics, in part because of people's reluctance to mix and use groundbaits for big fish - but you would be very unwise to dismiss it as a small fish technique.

LOADING A FEEDER

1. Fill the palm of your hand with groundbait, then place the empty feeder on top of the bait. Trial and error will tell you how much you need for different size feeders.

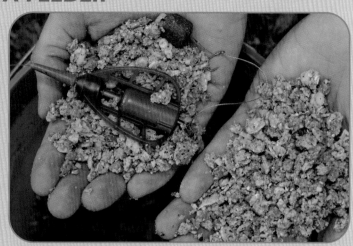

2. Fill your other palm with groundbait and push it over the top of the empty feeder and squeeze hard with both hands to mould it around the frame.

3. To compact and shape the Method ball keep the feeder in your left hand, alternately rotating the ball in your left hand and squeezing hard with the tips of your right fingers and heel of your palm.

4. The finished ball should be only slightly larger than the feeder, with none of the frame showing. Check it is a regular shape, smoothly finished and hanging centrally on the line.

5. Keep a small towel handy to wipe groundbait from your hands and prevent it getting on rods, reels and buzzers. Fox Micro Dry towels absorb more moisture than standard towels and pack away in a tiny pouch.

6. If you are receiving regular indications and they stop, wind in. The Method ball is probably gone, the hook bait picked up and ejected. Reload the feeder and recast. If it happens repeatedly change hook bait or length of your hook length.

"Every time a carp noses or attacks a method feeder you'll get an indication"

WHICH FEEDER?

FLATBED CARP FEEDER

ALTHOUGH sold under the Fox Match banner the Flatbed Carp Feeder design has applications for big carp as well as single and double-figure fish on commercial venues. Available in large and small sizes with loadings of 20 and 28 grams the Flatbed Feeder features a flat weighed base to prevent it rolling so readily when fishing up against sloping island margins. Smaller than most of the Fox Method and Maggot Method feeders they are a great choice where big carp have been battered on more standard size feeders, sitting discreetly inside a small ball of feed and offering a more subtle presentation.

METHOD FEEDER

IDEAL for big carp and specialist situations the Fox Method Feeder features a CAD designed translucent, camouflaged frame that alarms carp less when feeding around a partly broken down Method ball. The frame design retains groundbait effectively on the hardest casts, a rubber grommet securing a size 7 swivel for effective hooking with semi-fixed rigs. To allow hook baits to be tucked into the Method ball the feeder is weighted on one side, ensuring you can predict which way up it will always settle and position the hook bait on the top of the ball accordingly where it will produce takes the quickest. The Method Feeder is available in 14, 28, 35 and 60 grams.

MAGGOT METHOD FEEDER

AN innovative design from Fox the Maggot Method Feeder has an internal chamber that can be filled with maggots before the groundbait is moulded around the frame. Prolonging feeding around the Method ball it is perfect when using maggots for big carp. Alternatively, a foam insert for the central chamber is also supplied that can be dipped or soaked in liquid attractors that are released as fish feed on the Method ball. Long casting thanks to the bullet design nose the Maggot Method Feeder features a soft rubber insert for safe semi-fixed rigs and is available in six sizes from 20 grams through to 85 grams.

MIXING A METHOD GROUNDBAIT

THE correct consistency of groundbait is critical to successful Method feeder fishing. Too soft and the bait falls away from the feeder with minimal disturbance, failing to promote the aggressive attacking of the bait ball that underpins the success of the tactic. Too stiff and the lack of food reward from attacking the feeder works against you. Carp should have to work for the bait on the frame of the feeder rather than it falling off and breaking down in just a few minutes without any interference from feeding fish.

1. There are plenty of commercial Method groundbaits, but Vitalin Original dry dog food is cheap and makes great Method mixes. It resembles dry porridge and holds any number of other feed items to change texture, taste and smell.

2. Add a kilo of Vitalin and half a kilo of Mainline Pro-Active crushed tiger nut or crushed hemp stick mix to a bucket. Both improve the pull of your groundbait. The tiger nut mix is full of natural sugars helping create a stiffer mix.

3. Pellets are an essential addition, a couple of handfuls of small marine or shrimp pellets or Mainline Response Pellets. Always use small 2-4mm pellets. When water is added they break down and help bind the mix together more strongly.

5. Keep adding water and work the Vitalin around until it squeezes into a ball. If you can poke a finger in the groundbait without your finger getting dirty or the ball breaking it's the right consistency.

6. To finish your Method mix add a tin of tuna chunks in sunflower oil, draining the oil away first. A handful of sweetcorn adds a visual feed item to the mix and gives the option of plastic corn as a perfect hook bait.

7. Work the bait around the bucket or bowl again and leave it to stand for ten minutes. Check again that it squeezes into tough balls. Store it in a zip top bowl like the Evolution Method Bowl to stop it drying out.

METHOD GROUNDBAIT TRICKS

1. Adding Robin Red or a percentage of red groundbait darkens your mix down to spook carp less in clear, shallow water.

2. Peanut butter adds fantastic smell and taste, especially useful where particle baits are banned.

3. A splash of fish oil in your groundbait will ensure you see a flat spot on the surface as soon as there is any interest in your Method ball.

4. A tablespoon of chilli powder and the same of sea salt gives your groundbait a spicy twang for more action.

5. Don't add baits like hemp or mixed particle to your Method mix, the groundbait pulls the moisture out of them causing them to float.

4. Adding hot water binds Vitalin Method mix best. It's a job best done the night before or a few hours in advance. Start by adding two mugfuls of hot water from a kettle. A wooden mixing spoon makes it a cleaner job.

8. Regular casting will build bait in a swim but on many waters it can pay to feed more heavily. Use a Swinghead method catapult, medium/long range method catty or slingshot to feed your target area.

TOP TIP
There is a practical limit to the size of Method ball that can be cast out. But when using remote boats or dropping baits from rowing boats you can mould balls of bait the size of grapefruits or even bigger. Such a huge lump of food is something few carp have seen before and can be devastating.

TYING A METHOD FEEDER RIG

1. Loaded feeders can be very heavy. Always use minimum 15 lb main line when Method fishing.

2. Thread the required size feeder up the main line.

3. Tie the main line to the looped end of a Fox ready spliced lead core leader.

4. Push the feeder down on to the leader and locate the ring swivel in the rubber insert of the feeder.

5. Tie a short 10-15cm braided hook length to the ring swivel.

6. Load the feeder and you're ready to go.

CHAPTER 8

STALKING

STALKING

THE most intimate contest of all between angler and carp, stalking is not for the faint hearted. Being so close to feeding carp that you can see your hook bait on the bottom and watch every moment as a carp sucks it in, rights itself and bolts out of a swim is an adrenaline high from start to finish.

Where much of modern carp angling involves setting traps, stalking is a more mobile, aggressive tactic that creates opportunities to catch big carp in areas far off the beaten track and away from comfortable swims. Almost every lake will feature areas where carp routinely spend time to avoid the crashing and splashing of leads and marker floats. Often overgrown and inaccessible these are invariably areas where bivvies can't easily be pitched and two or three rods can't be fished.

But to the stalker, who travels lightly with just a single rod, net and unhooking mat and bare essentials these are areas where big carp can be caught unawares, and often remarkably easily. Stalking takes the game to the carp rather than waiting for them to come to you, but requires stealth. Wearing a white T-shirt, crashing around with heavy footfalls and talking loudly on a mobile phone is one way to guarantee you will never see let alone catch carp that you can see feeding just feet away.

HARDWARE

STALKING is no place for finesse. A carp taking the bait is often the start of an explosive battle at incredibly close quarters in confined areas where giving too much line is a recipe for a lost fish. Powerful and reliable tackle is essential.

Rods need to be short to make it easier to creep into out of the way areas. Standard 12 foot carbon rods can't be moved around easily when you're tucked in between bushes, and rods and line getting caught in vegetation could lead to disaster. The Fox Aquos Stalker at nine feet tucks into the tightest spots to present baits and features a progressive action right through to the butt to help cushion hook holds whilst exerting tremendous control on hooked fish under the rod tip. Small touches like double legged ringing, a keeper ring to retain rigs between swim moves and a short duplon handle for improved comfort and maximum manoeuvrability make it the perfect stalker's weapon.

Reels need to be rugged and robust with responsive clutches to guard against breakage when the pressure is piled on, yet small enough to balance with lightweight blanks. The Stratos FS7000 with 15+1 ball bearing operation, Supa Slow gear cycle and Slipper Stealth Clutch is the perfect choice. To withstand the inevitable knocks and scrapes when targeting carp in inaccessible spots reels should be loaded with 15 lb main line, choosing an abrasion resistant mono like Soft Steel Camo or Barbuster or 15 lb Illusion fluorocarbon.

TRIMMING DOWN TACKLE

KEEPING tackle at a minimum is essential. A few hours stalking can see you walking long distances and fighting in and out of undergrowth to feed spots and fish. You don't need rucksacks, carryalls, bivvies or barrows.

A small bag like the Evolution rig and bait carryall will hold everything you need. A bottle of drink, scales, sling, camera, bait and a small tackle box with a few spare leads, hook lengths, handful of rig bits plus baiting tools and scissors. Add a mat, net and rod and reel and you're ready to go. Look carefully at the tackle you routinely carry and weed out what you don't need such as spods, markers, spare spools, pods and alarms, cook kit and all the other session fishing trimmings.

IN THE JUNGLE

CARP know every inch of their environment and can find refuge in places many carpers would not dream of looking. When stalking all your fish catching opportunities are within feet of your own bank.

Look for any sort of cover, particularly overhanging trees, bushes and canopies of overhangs. Carp will often be tucked right underneath them, welcoming the sanctuary of snaggy branches and root systems that prevent anglers from fishing for them easily. Carp drift in and out of such areas regularly and have set routes that they follow, almost always along margins under your own feet. Such areas are often along overgrown banks and in less popular areas of a fishery where access is more difficult.

Baiting the edges of snaggy areas or large canopies is a good tactic, carp often dropping down to feed on the bait as they pass in and out of their safe haven. Other good areas to investigate are inlet and outlet pipes, cut throughs between different areas of a lake, monks, lily beds and shallows.

A handful or two of bait in any likely looking area gives plenty of options. Some areas might not be favoured by carp or contain any fish, others might be very productive indeed. Until you know a water well you are often playing a guessing game - laying the table for carp in lots of different places and waiting to see which area attracts their attention. Mentally note each area you have baited, and check each one of them in turn for signs of feeding carp.

Wherever you bait, make sure there is enough room for you to get into position with a rod, net and mat and then safely play and land a carp. With experience and the right tackle big fish can be landed from very tight spots but welfare comes first. Never introduce a rig in an area where you will be unable to land carp you hook.

FINDING FEEDING AREAS

1. On gravel pits areas of margin that carp frequent become 'polished' clean. Through polarising glasses productive areas of gravel margin often take on a distinctive yellow glow.

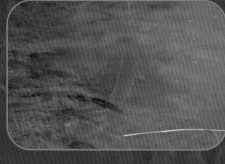

2. Where the water isn't clear enough to see the nature of the lake bed, gently lower a lead around in likely looking areas before baiting up. Areas carp are visiting will be hard bottomed, producing a donk on the rod tip as the lead touches down.

3. Push a boilie over the hook and lower a rig into likely areas and pull it gently along the bottom. If the end tackle collects foul smelling leaves and detritus you are unlikely to catch numbers of carp from the spot.

BAIT AND WAIT

EVEN during short sessions more time when stalking is spent without a bait in the water than actually fishing. Similar to successful surface fishing the key is to encourage carp to feed confidently before introducing a hook bait. Even a couple of hours without line and a rig in a swim builds incredible confidence in feeding carp - making them much more likely to make a mistake when the end tackle is eventually introduced.

Dependant upon the time of year, weather conditions, angler pressure and the spots you have baited it might only be minutes before the lake bed is covered in blue-grey shapes rooting around and hoovering up your free offerings or it may take several hours to interest just one or two fish. Patience and observation are two of the most valuable assets for the aspiring stalker.

THE EYES HAVE IT

GOOD underwater vision is more valuable when stalking than in any other carp fishing situation, making polarising glasses a vital piece of kit. Even short sessions can present varying light conditions in different areas of a lake, making the interchangeable lenses of the Fox Series 700 glasses indispensable.

In low light conditions of early and late in the day the amber lenses allow excellent visibility where darker lenses reduce rather than enhance your fish spotting capability. The colour of your lenses can make a huge difference to what you see.

Be aware it can take several minutes for your own vision to adjust for maximum underwater vision over each new baited area you visit. Polarising glasses also function less effectively when they are tilted. Therefore, try and maintain a level viewing position, and if you cannot see clearly, try moving your head very slightly from one side to the other to see if visibility improves - you might be pleasantly surprised what an effect a small change of viewing position has.

INTO POSITION

WHEN you spot fish feeding over one of your baited areas is when the adrenaline really starts to flow.

Patience remains crucial. Any jerky movements, heavy footfalls or standing up and skylining yourself can ruin your chances. Creep into position and watch carefully. Carp never feed intensively for long, and always drift away to chew what they have just eaten. When they drift away from the spot is the time to introduce an end tackle. The rig should be made up and baited, a PVA bag ready to slip over the hook, the clutch set only to give line when the rod is at maximum compression and the free spool tension tightened up not to give line too readily on the take.

End tackles should only ever be lowered off the rod top or with a gentle underarm swing to prevent a splash alarming carp nearby. Because you will be presenting a bait at such close quarters casting is never required.

If carp are feeding so hard that you can't introduce a rig without carp present, flick a tiny pinch of small pellets or hemp directly over the top of the fish. These light baits sinking around carp is often just enough to unsettle them to drift away briefly before returning to feed again - giving you a vital few seconds to lower a rig in.

Flick the free spool lever on, position the rod so the tip is only just poking out past the edge of the bank to make sure the line is sitting flush along the bottom and hanging down straight from the rod tip where it won't alarm carp unnecessarily. Now it's a waiting game. Get comfortable sitting on your mat, with rod and net next to your hand.

In clear water you will often see a carp hook itself against the lead, twisting and turning as it bolts from the swim, the rod tip pulling round and line being taken from the free spool. At such close quarters with a soft action rod and strong line you will be surprised how easily and quickly you can steer a carp into the net - often very little line needs to be given at all.

1. Small baits like hemp, pellets and chopped boilies encourage carp to feed for long periods, and return to an area repeatedly.

2. Most productive spots are within a couple of feet of the bank, allowing bait to be placed by hand. One good handful can keep carp feeding for up to a couple of hours.

3. Always feed Dynamite Frenzied Hemp. Because it is so oily bursts of oil droplets hitting the surface tell you a carp is feeding and disturbing your baited area below.

4. Slacken the line so it hangs limply from the rod top. Carp grubbing around can't help foul the line, tightening it gently before it falls slack again. Line bites are a great sign that a take is imminent.

"When you spot fish feeding over one of your baited areas is when the adrenaline really starts to flow"

CHAPTER 9

SNAG FISHING

FOX

SNAG FISHING

SNAGS can be anything from fallen trees and overhanging bushes to sunken fences, cars or discarded machinery from gravel workings. All have one thing in common - they attract carp like magnets.

The biggest threat carp know in their early life is predation from above the surface, and even as big fish they welcome cover over the top of their heads. In pressurised fishery environments any area that offers safety and sanctuary from anglers is also highly attractive.

From a fishery management point of view snags are a mixed blessing. It is good practice to allow carp areas to rest and lay up away from flying leads, spods and angler disturbance.

But too many snags reduce catches, carp choosing to stay within the safety of them for long periods rather than spending time in more accessible areas of a lake. Snags also increase the chances of anglers losing tackle and losing carp if they are fished incorrectly or by inexperienced carpers - which can lead to damaged fish.

Few venues, even reservoirs and man made commercial fisheries are without snags of some description, and being able to fish them safely and effectively - where allowed - is a valuable skill.

LOCKING UP

HOOKING and removing carp from the edges of snags is an explosive method, and requires you to give no line to carp on the take. Fishing with free spool systems in the usual way is a recipe for carp piling through snags and either shedding the hook or becoming snagged before you have a chance to pick up a rod. Even sitting over a rod for an instant strike isn't practical - carp have the element of surprise and lost fish are inevitable.

Fishing locked up the free spool system is kept off. When a fish is hooked and bolts it pulls the Hanger or Swinger up to the blank to give an audible indication from the buzzer but then meets solid resistance. Unable to take line the fish is forced to kite and is turned away from the snags. Stretch in the line acts as a cushion and even the biggest carp aren't able to generate enough momentum when bolting to break strong tackle on a direct pull. They are steered out from their sanctuary like a dog restrained on a lead.

The method depends upon the rod rest system rooting the rod, reel and buzzer securely enough to stop a carp pulling the rod in or the rests over, but executed correctly the hard part is done before you pick the rod up. It's an explosive tactic but it is a superbly efficient way of extracting carp safely from the densest snags.

1. Before putting the rod in the rests check the clutch of your reel is tightened right up and only gives line if maximum pressure is applied to the line on a straight pull. The free spool should be off.

2. Single bank sticks are the most secure option, or goal post Rod Lok bars. Duo Grip or Rod Lok rear rests grip the rods, stopping them being pulled in. Bank sticks should be firmly rooted with no back or forward motion possible.

3. Not all swims allow bank sticks to be rooted. Mini pod anchors slide over Stalker and Horizon pod legs and peg to the ground for stability. On platforms cup hooks can be screwed into boards and the elasticated pod stabiliser passed around the pod.

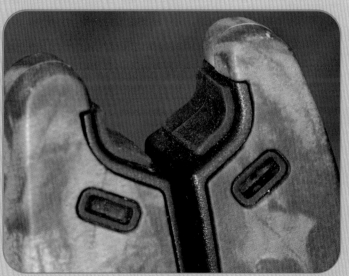

4. Rubber inserts on the inside of the vee in Micron and EOS series alarms also prevent rods being pulled forwards when a carp takes and positioning the butt ring of the rod in front of the alarm adds extra security against a rod being pulled off a rest.

BENEATH THE SURFACE

BEFORE casting a hook bait out it's essential to know the extent of a snag or underwater obstacle. What we see above the surface is often only a small part of a snag, especially when fishing swims containing fallen and overhanging trees. Casting tight to the edges of a snag that are visible above the water's surface is no guarantee that you are fishing safely or presenting baits effectively.

Polarising glasses will help see deeper into the water, picking out any obvious submerged branches or trunks that can guide you where to avoid placing baits. Always check if you can get closer to a snag than where you are fishing it from, it will give you a better look at how it sits underwater.

After using your eyes the only way to determine fishable areas is by using rod and line. Casting a bare lead around to feel the bottom and gently drawing it back towards you will tell you if the lake bed is smooth and fishable, or if there are branches or other potential snags that you can't see that will lead to losses or bad presentation. Use the 'creeping up' technique described in chapter 6 p98 to p99 to clip your line to stop yourself over casting and losing tackle in a snag, then exploring different areas to find likely positions for hook baits.

The golden rule is that you must keep hook baits on the outside edge of any snag. As carp become pressurised the closer a hook bait is fished to the edge of a snag the more productive it is likely to be, but you should never fish deep into snags where carp will be hooked only to be lost and left trailing tackle. You need to know where the dangers lie beneath the surface, not just the visible parts of a snag

Time spent in observation also gives vital clues as to which areas around a snag might be the most productive as well as the safest to fish. Watch the routes carp take when swimming in and out of the snag. Baits presented here stand the best chance of success. Often, where snags lie along margins, it is better to bait and fish where the margin meets the edge of the snag rather than the outer edges of a snag that sit further out into the lake.

DIRECTION DANGERS

ALTHOUGH when locked up carp are unable to take line and plough directly back into snags, hooked fish will still kite left or right, causing problems if swims are not chosen carefully to offer the safest angle to pressure carp away.

In the first instance fishing directly across to the left hand edge of a snag tree allows hooked carp to kite to the right, still allowing carp to make the sanctuary of the submerged branches, a recipe for lost fish and tackle failure. In the second example, by setting up further around the bank and fishing at a different angle, hooked carp can't take line to make it back into the snags and if kiting are still pressured away from the snags - a much safer option.

HOOKED CARP CAN STILL KITE DEEPER INTO SNAGS EVEN IF NO LINE IS GIVEN

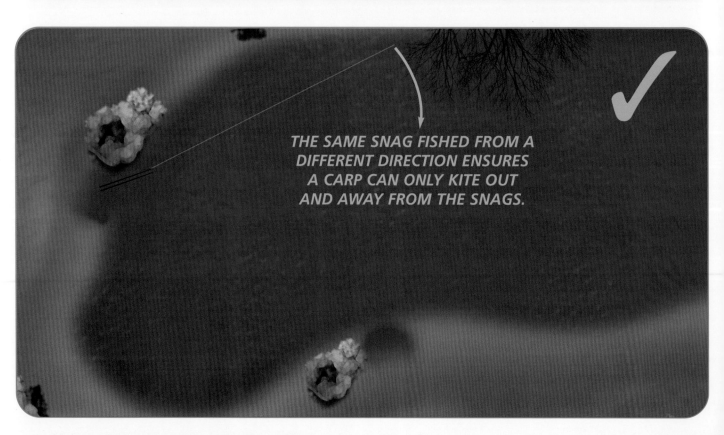

THE SAME SNAG FISHED FROM A DIFFERENT DIRECTION ENSURES A CARP CAN ONLY KITE OUT AND AWAY FROM THE SNAGS.

INDICATION

SNAG fishing demands instant and effective indication. Setting Hangers or Swingers incorrectly delays how quickly a take is registered at the rods and in extreme circumstances can allow carp to take too much line and become snagged even if the free spool is knocked off and the clutch gives no line.

Although slack line fishing is fashionable to minimise the chances of carp spooking on the sight and feel of line passing through a swim, it's not recommended for snag work. Indication is very effective with slack lines but the extra line paid out gives carp a greater chance of making it into snags before hitting the resistance of a rod and reel fished locked up.

Hangers or Swingers should be fished on a drop of just a couple of inches. With buzzers set to their most sensitive. This allows several bleeps as the line pulls the indicator tight up to the blank, but doesn't allow carp any additional movement before hitting a solid wall of resistance and being forced to kite. Drop back bites are also increasingly likely when snag fishing, and at anything beyond short ranges additional drag weights on indicators close to the rod give effective indication of slack line bites.

Adding Fox Dual Line Clips to the rod butt immediately behind the indicator also enhances indication, ensuring the smallest movements are registered quickly.

TOP TIP

AIM to snag fish with your rods pointing as directly as possible to the hook bait and rig. Fishing at acute angles allows carp several feet movement when the rod tip is pulled around on the take and delays indication.

If you are forced into acute angles at the rod tip by the layout of a swim push an additional three or four foot storm rod in around the middle spigot in front of the buzzer and tight to the blank. It acts as a barrier preventing the rod being pulled off the rests on a violent take.

"Ensure the smallest movements are registered by using Fox Dual Line Clips together with a good quality buzzer"

"A carp should already be turned away from a snag by the time you pick the rod up"

LINE

ALTHOUGH braided lines offer improved indication because of their lack of stretch, their abrasion resistance is a fraction of that of monofilament. It makes for a tough choice - do you want the faster indication of a braided line but poorer abrasion resistance in the event of the line contacting a branch or choose less instant indication from mono but greater resilience from your tackle? Opinions vary but reliable, highly abrasion resistant 15 lb monos like Barbuster or Soft Steel are the most popular choice. Fluorocarbons are also highly abrasion resistant and 15 lb Illusion makes another highly effective main line choice for snag situations, having the advantage of reduced stretch and visibility and sitting lower in the water.

STRIKING AND PLAYING

THE first few moments of a battle are crucial when snag fishing. With confidence in the safety of your bankside set up and the strength of your tackle there should be no doubts that as soon as your alarm sounds you will be shortly netting a carp, not fearing disaster.

Fishing locked up a carp should be already turned or being pressured away from a snag by the time you even pick up a rod. The pressure you exert after you pick the rod up should simply keep a carp moving and steer it to open water.

The first 10-15 seconds after the take is registered are the most crucial. Where space allows, applying maximum sidestrain as soon as the rod is picked up from the rests helps keep a carp off balance. Sweep the rod back as far as possible, quickly winding down to keep contact with the carp, and repeating several times to gain line quickly and pressure the carp to safety.

The clutch should be left alone, no line should be given, and only when several turns of line have been gained and a carp is swimming out from the snags should you consider flicking the anti-reverse off to play a fish on backwind or slackening the clutch to give line as required through the rest of the fight.

Alternatively, if the nature of the swim allows, immediately after picking up the rod wind down hard to the carp and then walk slowly and steadily backwards up the bank to keep a carp moving towards you. Once you've walked five or ten yards the carp should be well away from danger, now wind down and continue to play the fish as usual.

TOP TIP
IT is never more important to routinely check your main line, leaders or tubing and hook lengths for damage than when snag fishing. The slightest brush with a snag can considerably weaken line and terminal tackle. After catching a carp run your fingers along the last rod length of line and inspect the end tackle for nicks and abrasions. If in doubt remove any line that may have been weakened and re-tie end tackles and hook lengths.

"Win the first few moments of the battle, and the rest should be easy"

SAFE SNAG TACKLE

HIGHLY abrasion resistant end tackles prevent unnecessary losses when a line or rig contacts any subsurface obstacle, whether branches, pillars or posts. But using tough tackle needs to be weighed against carp safety.

No matter how strong the lines and rig components in use there is always a danger of tackle failure. No responsible angler ever intends to lose tackle or suffer breakages but it can happen, even to experienced carpers.

The nature of snag fishing results in an increased chance of tackle failure. No lines can easily withstand the slicing of razor sharp mussels festooned on sunken branches or being run across tough flints. It's important to ensure end tackles are as safe as possible in the event of any breakages.

Keep lead core leaders short. Lead core is universally popular, its tough polyester coating providing increased protection from abrasions and nicks that might otherwise cut

through the main line during a fight. But it has become increasingly common to see leaders of six, eight and ten feet in use to extend that protection and guard against tackle failure in snaggy swims. Such long leaders are unnecessary, and can be potentially dangerous. The tougher you make the material a carp is attached to the less chance it has got of ridding itself of that tackle following a breakage and the more of it there is the greater the chances that it will become entangled.

15 lb Fox Camo Soft Steel or Illusion fluorocarbon main line.

Two small blobs of Hi-SG putty can be moulded around the main line around 15 and 30 inches above the lead core leader to help keep the main line flush to the lake bed for improved tackle concealment.

A ready spliced 450mm 45 lb lead core leader with ring swivel sits the line behind the rig tight to the bottom and offers improved abrasion resistance where the end tackle is most at risk.

A 2-3 oz flat swivel pear lead stopped by a knot protector bead ensures more instant indication than semi-fixed leads when a carp tightens the hook length. Running leads are also the safest, most carp friendly end tackles.

Running lead rigs also allow cobweb PVA bags to be slipped over the hook prior to casting to prevent tangles and to tightly group free offerings around the hook bait.

RECOMMENDED SNAG RIG

CARP are often much more confident feeders round snags, allowing end tackles to be kept simple and efficient. Tangle free casting and fast, effective indication of a take using strong, reliable components are the priority.

Long lead core leaders kink readily, making it much more difficult for leads and rig bits to be jettisoned in the event of a main line failure. Lead core is also a much higher breaking strain than reel lines, giving a carp little or no chance of ridding itself of a long leader that becomes entangled in snags. Sticking to lead core end lengths of up to 18 inches still provides valuable protection to the line at most risk behind a hooked carp but maintains rig safety.

Anti-tangle tubing is another safe alternative for snag end tackles. Tubing is highly abrasion resistant, and has the added advantage that in the event of breakages lines pull freely through tubing and associated rig bits. With responsible end tackle construction that often leaves carp only trailing a hook length and a length of mono.

Although rarely required in the UK, in extreme environments such as found on many Continental venues

where huge rocks and sunken tree stumps can be encountered a snag leader is advisable. A Fox Armadillo leader of between five and seven metres boosts abrasion resistance immediately behind the end tackle, casts smoothly and thanks to its low diameter knots to heavy mono reel lines neatly with a double grinner knot or Mahin knot.

Try this if you're fishing a very snaggy venue and need the extra protection a snag leader will offer.

Free offerings should be scattered around the rig - baiting deeper inside the snags where carp can't be caught only encourages them to feed hard where you have no chance of catching them.

A Coretex combi link with a small section of coating peeled back behind the hook offers effective presentation, pinned down with small blobs of Hi-SG tungsten putty to prevent spooking carp.

An Arma Point SSC offers tremendous hooking and holding power, staying firmly in even as a carp hits the resistance of a locked up rod and reel on the take. A small angled shrink tube extension provides even more aggressive hooking.

CHAPTER 10

"Catching big carp on floating baits is one of the most intense methods of all"

FLOATER FISHING

CARP love nothing more than to cruise the upper layers in the summer, enjoying the warmth and looking for food.

There's plenty of natural food on or near the surface, everything from hatching flies to snails and even silver birch tree catkins that they suck to remove the seeds. Even the most inexperienced carper will have seen carp slurping or mouthing at items on the surface to either eat or identify if they are edible.

Catching big carp on floating baits is one of the most intense methods of all. The anticipation as you watch fish wolfing down free offerings around your bait is electric, and the explosive boil as a carp makes a mistake, takes the hook bait and the rod hoops over is more exciting than any buzzer sounding.

Floater fishing demands patience and observation. Unlike fishing on the bottom you can see how the carp are behaving and see how close you are to catching. You'll never be in any doubt if there are any feeding fish in front of you.

Surface fishing is hugely neglected on most venues. On blazing hot days it's common to find anglers watching carp on the surface in front of them with baits still fished on the bottom rather than switching to floating baits. It makes big opportunities for those who bother to target carp in the upper layers.

PERFECT PELLETS

CARP can be caught on all manner of floating baits from lumps of bread crust to sunflower seeds and even marshmallows.

For years the standard issue surface bait has been floating dog biscuits, but they have little to offer other than availability and price and there are better alternatives. The most reliable floating bait of all is the floating trout pellet, widely available either in kilo bags from bait manufacturers or bulk from feed and grain merchants or a nearby trout farm. If you feed dog biscuits and pellets together you'll see the carp eat the pellets in preference, and feeding only dog biscuits reduces the level of feeding activity. Dog and cat biscuits can be flavoured and softened to make them more attractive and individual to you but carp still seem to much prefer pellets straight out of the bag. No contest - pellets are the only floating bait you need on most venues. A combination of fish and vegetable proteins, fish oils and appetite stimulators they are as keenly accepted as marine and trout pellets on the bottom.

Being shelf-life a bag or two of floating trout pellets can also be left in a rucksack or car for use at a moment's notice rather than floaters having to be prepared or defrosted each trip on the off chance you'll use them. Widely available in 4, 6 and 11mm a mix of all the sizes will encourage even tricky carp to feed hard, the largest size being perfect for on the hook.

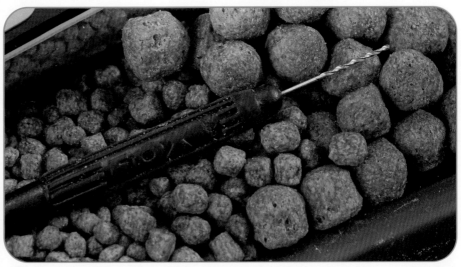

FEEDING

The biggest single mistake any keen carp angler makes is to repeatedly cast floating hook baits straight at carp that are visible on the surface. It's rare a carp will take a floating bait cast on its nose.

You ultimately catch more surface feeding carp by not fishing for them, and spending time feeding a swim. Unless you are trying to catch an individual fish or two that you can see up close it's always wise to gradually introduce free offerings and let carp spend time eating undisturbed in the swim and build in both greed and confidence before trying to catch them. Drift a few baits out over their heads and keep a careful eye on how they react. On a good day they may eat them straight away. But most days on most venues it will take some time and a steady introduction of freebies to encourage carp to feed. Patience is crucial, feeding a swim until carp are competing for free offerings will pay dividends rather than being impatient and unsettling carp before they have really begun feeding with abandon.

On difficult venues it may take all afternoon and evening feeding a swim before casting out late in the day for a good chance of a fish as the light fades. It's too much effort for some, but in the same period of time with baits on the bottom you would often have caught nothing.

The more of a carp's head you see pushing out of the water as it eats floating baits the more confident it is. When you see fish eating one floater and then staying on the surface to greedily mop up a second or even third free offering nearby it's time to cast out. Lob the controller past the feeding area, gently wind it back into the centre of the activity, and often it will only take seconds for a carp to boil at the hook bait. Normally, semi-fixed controllers will do the hooking for you. Wait for the float to move or the main line to tighten, lift the rod - fish on!

"At longer range spod floating pellets or catapult cobweb bags filled with pellets and stones"

GETTING THE DRIFT OF IT

GOOD observation followed by practical swim choice are two of the most important things to get right. You can have the most attractive bait, an effective rig and get carp feeding but without paying attention to wind and drift across a swim the result can be very poor presentation and little chance of catching.

It's important to position yourself so the wind is coming over your shoulder and slightly across you. It makes drifting free offerings over fish easier without having to fire them on their heads and makes it as easy as possible to keep the line straight to the controller rather than letting it be pulled in a big bow. Keep the main line straight to keep the float and hook bait drifting at the right speed with the free offerings.

Flicking the rod up and mending the line is a vital skill, preventing the wind pulling the float and hook bait unnaturally.

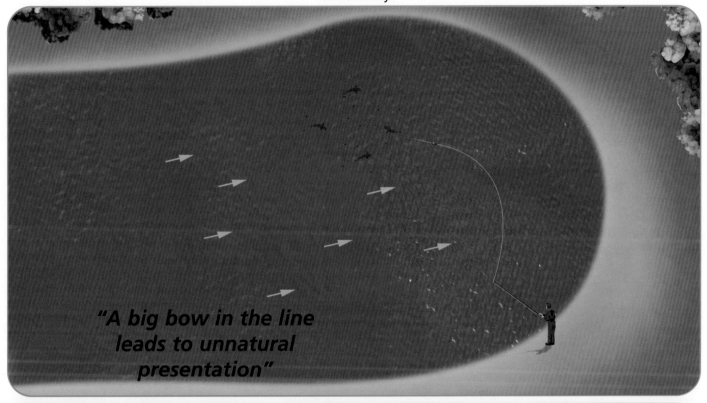

"A big bow in the line leads to unnatural presentation"

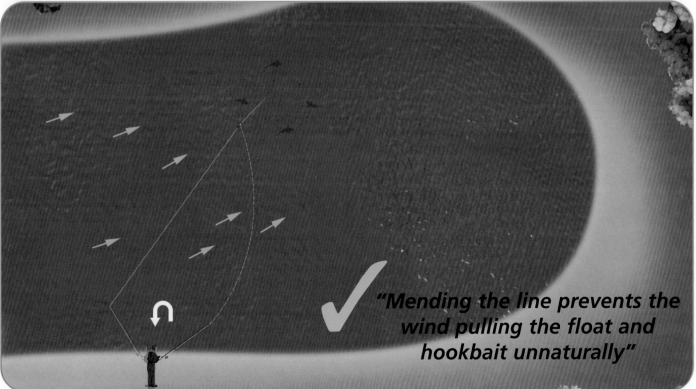

"Mending the line prevents the wind pulling the float and hookbait unnaturally"

BRAID OR MONO?

AS with reel line choice for fishing on the bottom and reel lines choice for spodding, opinion is split over the merits of braided Dyneema versus mono for surface fishing.

Dyneema is a naturally buoyant material. Using a braided reel line for surface fishing ensures the reel line floats without needing to be treated. Braid sits high in the surface film, allowing it to be easily lifted up and line to be mended for correct drift of a controller and presentation of a hook bait.

Its low diameter also helps cast controllers long distances easily. In experienced hands it makes fine control of floater tackle effortless. In turn this aids the presentation of your hookbait and undoubtedly results in more bites.

On the down side its lack of stretch leaves little room for errors and when using fine, low diameter hook lengths an over enthusiastic strike or violent take can leave you with a breakage rather than a carp in the net.

Fox Controller Floater Braid has a knot strength of 12 lb and is designed to resemble floating weed for absolute camouflage, its low diameter making casting even lightweight controllers or even freelined baits effortless.

In inexperienced hands braided lines on the surface are best avoided. Soft Steel Camo is the best mono choice for a floater fishing main line, its alternating sections of different colours effectively breaking up the outline of your tackle, spooking fish less readily.

All floater fishing main lines need to float or as line gradually sinks between controller and rod tip it pulls the hook bait out of position. Feeding carp that feel or see subsurface line around them will also spook very easily.

Either load and pack a spare spool of 10 or 12 lb Soft Steel Camo that is treated with line floatant and used only for surface fishing or alternatively run your line back through a pad of silicone line floatant or Vaseline before commencing surface fishing. Whichever you choose, your main line must float for effective surface presentation.

"Fox Controller Floater Braid is designed to resemble floating weed"

WHICH CONTROLLER?

CONTROLLERS fall into two distinct categories, upright floats and in-line models. Both designs have specific uses.

The new Fox Exocet model is an upright design with a short, dumpy shape for bolt effect. A vaned body and aerodynamic weighted base makes it a very long casting, accurate controller, the clear finish preventing carp from spooking unnecessarily from the float. The smallest 5 and 10 gram versions are excellent for pin point accuracy at shorter ranges, making a minimal disturbance when entering the water. The two largest 15 and 20 gram models make great medium to long range floats, allowing you to present baits at up to 80 yards in the right conditions. The large high-viz orange sight tip ensures you are always able to track the hook bait even in difficult light.

In-line floats are popular for pressurised fish, a less distinct shape sitting in the surface film rather than above and below it spooking cagey fish less readily. The Fox in-line Bolt Bubble floats are weight forward opaque plastic floats that can be part filled with water for casting weight to create maximum bolt effect and prick a fish when the hook length is tightened. They don't cast long distances as readily as the Exocets, but offer a tremendously subtle presentation with very little on show to alarm a carp and provide excellent self-hooking. Because they have a translucent finish, sit low in the surface film and are part filled with water they are more difficult to see with the human eye too, and are suited to shorter ranges and good light conditions. But such is their hooking efficiency you are normally fishing for carp that bolt after meeting the resistance of the float.

"The new Fox Exocet Float is suited to long range work. The Bolt Bubble is better for shorter work or when targeting cagey fish"

"The finer your hook length the more takes you get when floater fishing"

TYING A CONTROLLER RIG

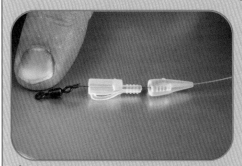

1. Thread your Soft Steel Camo main line or Floater Controller Braid through the tail rubber and clear safety clip supplied with Fox Exocet controllers and tie on a size 10 swivel.

2. Pull the swivel into the safety clip, then add the controller and secure with the tail rubber. Exocets are available in 5, 10, 15 and 20 grams. Surface feeding carp quickly drift further away from you when you cast out so pick at least one size heavier than you think you need.

3. The finer your hook length the more takes you get when floater fishing but getting takes has to be balanced against landing carp safely. Use 8 or 10 lb Soft Steel hook lengths in open water. Near weed or snags stick to 12 and even 15 lb Soft Steel.

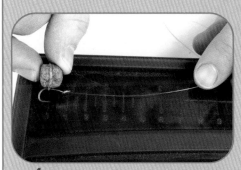

4. The length of your hook length is also crucial. An eight or ten foot hook length can often get more takes than a six foot link. Start at eight feet and be prepared to go longer to keep the bait further away from the controller.

5. Small hooks get more bites than big patterns because they are less visible and weigh the hook bait down less but they need to be strong enough to land big carp. For open water tie a size 8 or 10 Fox Series 2 direct to the hook length or for tougher situations a size 8 or 9 Arma Point SSSP.

6. You can drill and hair rig or glue most floating hook baits but when using pellets the most reliable method for great presentation every time is a latex bait band. Pass the hook through the small rubber extension on the edge of the band and using a dab of rig glue fix it in place slightly forwards of where the point is opposite the shank.

7. Floating 11mm trout pellets are a great hook bait. There's huge variation in size and shape of trout pellets within a packet, look for the longer pellets as hook baits. Lightly score them around the centre with rig scissors to create a shallow groove and then slip them into the band so the band sits in the groove.

8. The hook length needs to be lightly greased so it sits on the surface film. If the hook length sinks it drags the hook bait slowly towards the controller and the line at eye level to a surface cruising carp is alarming.

9. Always test the hook bait by dropping it in the margins and seeing how it sits before casting out. The hook should be neatly under the pellet, point downwards. Between casts and after each fish check that the band hasn't slipped around the shank.

ALTERNATIVE HOOK BAITS
CORK

Carp quite happily mop up pieces of cork on the surface, its big advantage that it can't soften and be knocked or pulled off the hook or hair by carp playing with the hook bait. If using floating pellets try hair rigging a length of 6mm cork stick as supplied with Fox Nut Drills. For mixer fishing try direct hooking a cork ball, making sure all of the hook point is proud.

ARTIFICIAL MIXERS

A new addition to the mass of artificial baits available, plastic mixers are a soft, rubbery imitation bait that can be direct hooked. You can hook one at the start of the day and leave it on all day which makes them incredibly convenient. Fake mixers also feature a small recess in one side that takes a small split shot. As long as you hook the side opposite the split shot it flips the bait over, keeping the hook above the surface where carp can't see or feel it and can bring bonus takes.

POP-UPS

Most of us routinely carry pop-ups, and they can be hair rigged to use amongst floating baits.
Warmer colours like pink and yellow are highly visible making it easier to keep an eye on the hook bait.
Most pop-ups float indefinitely and won't soften and come off the rig. Vastly different in colour, size and smell to your free offerings pop-ups can sometimes work well with carp homing in on them first, but can also be too obvious and spook fish easily. Try them but don't rely on them.

TOP TIP

MANY surface fishing opportunities arise in warm weather and strong sunshine. The brighter the sunshine the more clearly carp see your tackle. Hooks themselves can be clearly visible and put carp on edge as much as line. Try adding a thin coat of Tippex to the shank and the bend of the hook, but leave the length of the point uncoated so as not to impair hooking. When viewed from underneath against strong sunshine a white hook is less obvious to a carp, bringing bonus takes.

"Most of us routinely carry pop-ups, and they can be hair-rigged to use amongst floating baits. Warmer colours like pink and yellow are highly visible and make it easier to keep an eye on the hook bait"

BEATING THE BIRDS

BIRD life can be irritating on some venues, and in extreme circumstances make surface fishing almost impossible. If you are having problems with birds mopping up your floaters try spooling up with TB Spod Braid instead of Controller Floater Braid. The bright yellow colour of Spod Braid is enough to alarm most birds and keep them away from your hook bait. Being light coloured viewed against the brightness of the sky, carp aren't spooked any more by such a high-vis line than by a sombre finish main line.

Also, remember feeding carp are enough to spook birds away, so keep feeding the swim. Using a spod to introduce the free offerings also alarms bird life much more than it does the carp, keeping them away from your baited area.

"The bright yellow colour of Spod Braid is enough to alarm most birds and keep them away from your hook bait"

ZIG RIGGING

ZIG rigging is a method of presenting buoyant hook baits anywhere in the upper layers to catch opportunist carp that are cruising around rather than feeding hard on the bottom. Also referred to as suspended baits, they are exactly that - buoyant hook baits suspended somewhere between the lake bed and the surface.

No matter how attractive your bait and effective your rig if carp are cruising around a couple of feet below the surface you won't catch them on baits fished on the bottom.

Even difficult or wary carp often just eat a piece of food stuck in front of their nose rather than swim around it. Zig rigging has become a mainstream method, and each season accounts for huge carp. It's a tactic that requires confidence, but can be responsible for great catches.

To many the idea of casting a single small pop-up into a lake and expecting a carp to find it and eat it is just too much. But there's much more to zig rigging than that.

WHEN?

ZIG rigging scores in all sorts of different conditions. Generally, on hot days through the spring and summer months carp will often be found near to the surface.

With polarising glasses you will see dark shapes or the distinctive V shaped bow waves as carp move along under the surface.

Zig rigs can score all year round, but spring and summer are excellent times. In the spring carp are quickly up to the surface for the first few really hot spells, shaking off the hangover of winter and enjoying the warmth of the sun.

They will often be found in corners or bays that are sun traps, or be seen cruising along bars and around island margins. During high summer carp routinely spend long periods in the upper layers, whether basking, simply getting about from place to place or feeding on emerging insect life.

But there are no hard and fast rules as to when carp will get caught on zig rigs. Sometimes when conditions seem perfect for red letter days on bottom baits with thick cloud, big winds and carp crashing everywhere it can be zig rigs fished well off bottom that produce the only action. Surprisingly to some even in the depths of winter carp can also be caught on baits fished well off bottom. Be prepared to fish up in the water for them whenever the opportunity arises.

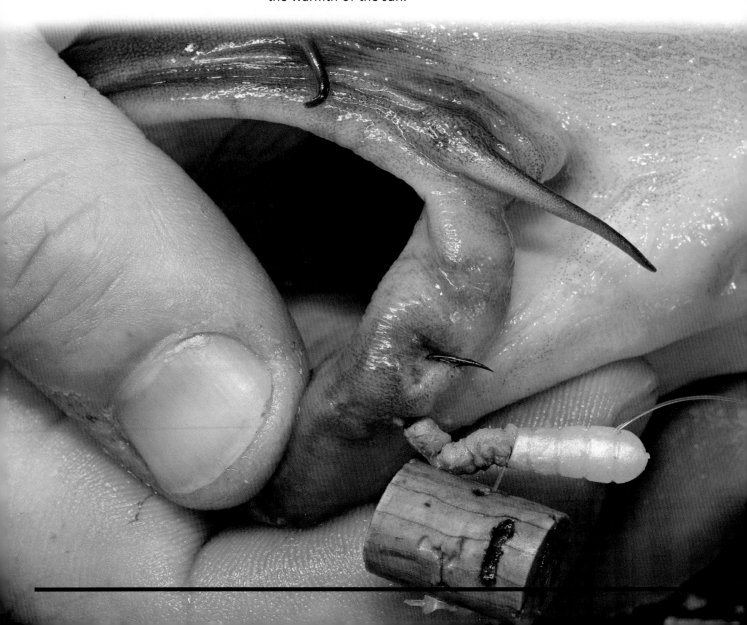

TYING A ZIG RIG

1. You can either use a simple running lead or a semi-fixed lead arrangement - there's little to choose between them although the running rig is more sensitive. For semi-fixed set-ups an in-line lead reduces tangles. A ring swivel also reduces the chance of tangles.

2. Avoid anti-tangle tubing and leaders, the hook length will often be so much longer than any length of tubing or lead core that it makes them redundant. With long hook lengths a shorter leader or length of tubing also creates a potential tangle point where it joins the main line.

3. The finer your hook length is when zig rigging the more bites you get. But it has to be balanced against successfully landing carp. Use 8 or 10 lb links in open water, 12 and 15 lb around thick weed or snags. Illusion fluorocarbon is the perfect choice because of its reduced visibility.

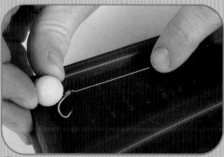

4. Hooks should be small so they are less easily detected but with a wide gape for efficient hooking. Arma Point SSSP or SSBP patterns in sizes 7-10 are ideal. Tie them direct to your hook length material.

5. After finding the depth of the area you want to fish, tie the link so it is one to two feet shorter, presenting your hook bait one to two feet below the surface. Measuring off against the lid of a Fox Box makes it easier to be accurate.

6. Fox Hair Widgets make it easy to tie effective zigs every time. Push the Widget over the hook point and slide it around the bend and shank until it sits just above the eye. Using fine braid tie a hair to the central groove that is 2-3mm longer than the bait you intend to use.

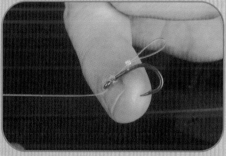

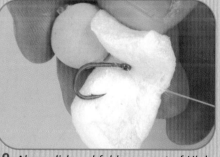

7. The hook needs to be sat tight underneath the bait, so the point is pushed upwards for earlier hooking when a carp takes the bait. Never have more than a few millimetres clearance between the hook and the bottom of the bait.

8. Alternatively use a knotless knot, whipping just three or four turns so the hair exits just above the eye, although with long hook lengths it can be fiddly to pass six or eight feet of line down through the eye. Again, keep the hair short, long hairs and hairs exiting from further up the hook shank lead to dropped takes and hook pulls.

9. Always lick and fold a nugget of High Riser Foam around the hook before casting. It helps prevent tangles in flight and makes it much easier to watch the hook bait in flight so you are confident the rig lands tangle free.

10. A finished zig rig is very straight forward, a lead, bead, ring swivel and hook length tied long enough to sit in the upper layers of the swim you are fishing. It's not the most efficient hooking arrangement and depends upon carp taking the bait and swimming off with it, but zigs remain incredibly productive.

HOW DEEP?

HOW do you know how long to make your hook length when tying up a zig rig? Unless you know a venue very well you'll need to plumb a swim to gauge the depth so you know how deep to set your hook bait. When carp are cruising around it's normally possible to sneak a cast in when fish have drifted away to another part of a swim. One cast with a small lead and micro marker is enough, feeding the float up and accurately measuring the depth. Retrieve the float and then measure off a hook length to tie your zig up.

In warmer weather start with a hook bait one or two feet below the surface, but be prepared to experiment. If there are good numbers of fish cruising around don't be shy of trying one zig below the surface and another at half depth. Carp can be caught at any level between the lake bed and the surface depending upon conditions.

"Fox Marker Float Rods have depth markers on the blank to help ensure a more accurate reading"

FOOD TRAPS
Anywhere that a scum or film collects on the surface often attracts carp underneath, nosing round for food.

BARS AND ISLANDS
Look for routes that carp are patrolling regularly, along bars or out from the tip of islands.

MARGINS
Any inaccessible margins with tree cover, marginal weed or lilies will have carp patrolling along them, often in the upper layers.

WHERE TO FISH ZIG RIGS

X X

X

BAYS
Bays often act as sun traps and X
attract carp cruising around
through the daytime.

X

X X

X

PLATEAUX
Carp often collect on top large
underwater features like plateaux.
Zigs placed on top of them or
alongside them score well.

BITE TIME

Takes vary tremendously when zigging. Commonly you will either get spool spinning one-toners but with semi-fixed leads small drop backs are also positive takes and should always be struck. With running leads a slow tightening of the line, lifting of the bobbin or shakes on the rod tip can also often mean a carp has hooked itself. To improve indication always try and point the rod directly at the hook bait, using single bank sticks if necessary. If there is action to be had on zig rigs it normally comes very quickly after casting - be warned!

CASTING ZIGS

ZIG rigging involves casting much longer hook lengths than we would ever normally use when bottom fishing. Such a long length of line hanging below the lead can be difficult to cast. Any movement of the lead before the cast is magnified at the bait and it's easy to get the hook length caught in trees or vegetation bordering the swim.

The easy solution is to cast the hook bait from off the ground. Position the lid from your tub of High Riser Foam or a bucket lid on the ground directly under the rod tip. Lick and squeeze a nugget of foam around the hook and put it on the lid.

Being careful not to move the hook bait from the lid, position the lead below the rod tip so it has the same drop as when you cast standard end tackles. Check that the hook length line hanging slack between lead and hook bait isn't caught on anything then cast as usual, aiming slightly higher for a smooth tangle-free flight. Links as long as 10-12 feet can be cast trouble free in this manner. Feather the cast as the rig nears the water and you should see two plops when the rig touches down, the lead followed by the hook bait.

FEEDING

IT can be a great tactic to feed floating baits over the top of a zig rig. Often we rely on carp falling for effectively a single hook bait fished under the surface but regular feeding with floaters such as trout pellets or cat biscuits over a zig can produce spectacular results, allowing you to target carp on the surface at ranges well beyond those that you can effectively fish with controller and standard surface tactics.

Zig end tackles with heavy leads can be cast long distances and spods with floating pellets can comfortably be cast 100 yards on the right tackle. Because the hook bait is anchored subsurface by a heavy lead it's also unaffected by drift unlike controllers fished at range that require constant mending of the main line to achieve good presentation. Regular spodding over the hook bait should sooner rather than later result in a one-noter on the zig fished a foot or two beneath the freebies. When spodding floating pellets there is no better hook bait than a small length of 6mm cork stick.

HOOK BAIT CHOICES

CARP fall for all sorts of hook baits fished subsurface. Pop-ups are the obvious choice, and small, bright baits a common choice. Stick to 14mm and smaller, with yellow, white and red all scoring well. Trimming the edges away from the baits with scissors so your hook bait isn't round is a good trick to bring extra bites.

Cork or foam is also an excellent choice. A hair rigged length of 6mm cork stick or a cork ball catch plenty of carp, even when fished on their own with no feeding of free offerings. A section of brightly coloured foam as supplied with the Fox Boilie Punch is also a great hook bait for zigging.

There's a huge confidence barrier to overcome casting out a piece of cork or foam on a zig rig and expecting a carp to eat it with no other feed items around.

Remember carp have to take an item into their mouth to see if it is food and decide whether they want to eat it or reject it. Artificial hook baits like cork and foam often outscore the commonly used pop-up hook baits on zigs simply because carp don't associate non-food, unflavoured items with danger the way they do strongly smelling, bright balls.

"There's a huge confidence barrier to overcome casting out a piece of cork or foam and expecting a carp to eat it with no other feed items around it"

A hook is often visible to a carp approaching a zig in clear water and good light. Threading artificials like small rubber worms around the bend disguises the hook, making it look more interesting and edible to a carp.

CHAPTER 11

WINTER FISHING

FOX

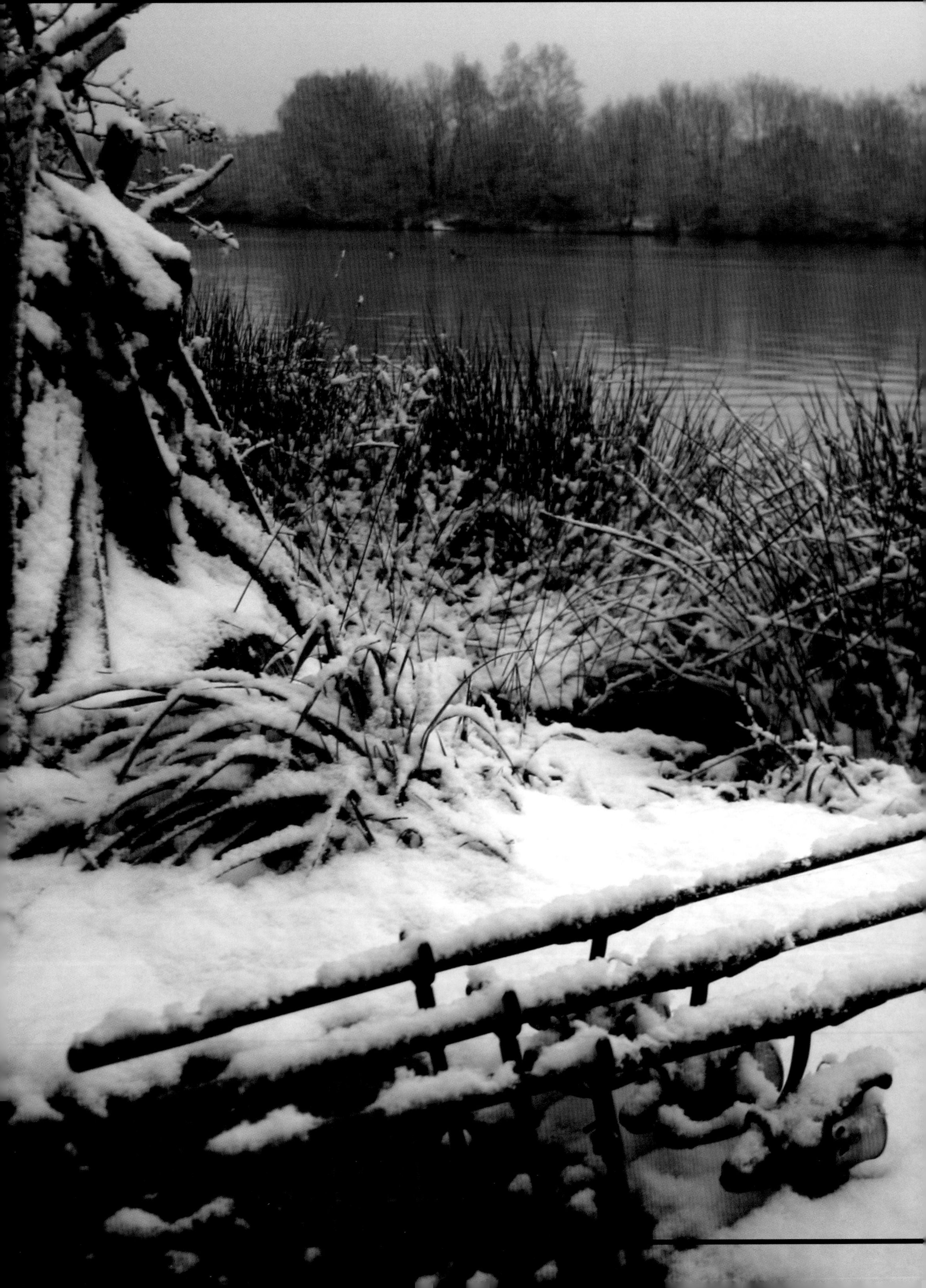

WINTER FISHING

WHERE carp were once thought to be uncatchable through the winter months and carp rods were routinely swapped for pike rods when the first frosts arrived we have long since known that carp continue to be active at regular intervals right through the calendar. Carp can be caught in the snow, and even from under ice during freeze ups.

But our climate has changed significantly and with it the behaviour of carp through the seasons of the year. Where October and November once marked the arrival of very cold weather, frosts, ice and snow, the onset of winter is now characterised more by wet and windy weather, leaving water temperatures higher for longer and carp more active.

With well stocked carp waters more readily available than ever before it's never been easier to catch winter carp. Carp become different creatures through the colder months, with deep, rich colours ranging from chestnut brown across their backs to vibrant yellows and oranges on their fins and undersides. There is little as pleasurable as playing, landing and photographing such good looking fish on a crisp winter's day.

THE NUMBERS GAME

CARP waters vary tremendously in difficulty, stocking level and potential rewards. The more lightly stocked a venue the less likely it is to produce well in the winter months. The most reliable sport comes from venues with high stock densities where there is increased competition for food. On a big fish water containing just a few dozen carp there might be no fish prepared to feed for several days, weeks or even months.

In contrast on a venue containing 1,000 carp even if only a tiny percentage of the stock is prepared to feed on any given day it still swings the odds considerably in your favour. On the right venue multiple catches can be common through the winter, just as in the warmer months.

Targeting well stocked venues doesn't mean sacrificing the chances of a big fish. There are plenty of club and day ticket waters that contain good numbers of doubles and 20 lb fish and offer the genuine chance of a 30-pounder.

Even commercial complexes that are tailored more towards match and pleasure anglers often contain good numbers of doubles and odd 20-pounders and make excellent venues for some cold water carp action. The disturbance of numbers of anglers, regular casting and continued bait availability on these venues is another great help encouraging carp to remain active through the bitterest conditions

Winter can also be a good time to look for carp in stretches of rivers and canals where flow and boat traffic continues to keep carp active and catchable in the coldest conditions.

"The most reliable winter sport comes from venues with high stock densities where there is increased competition for food"

TOP TIP
A BIG percentage of winter action on well stocked venues comes quickly after recasting. Use one rod to recast every half hour to an hour with a fresh high attract pop-up or dipped bait to try and locate carp in different areas of a swim. Continue to fish any area if it produces a fish - more action shouldn't be far away.

LOCATING WINTER CARP

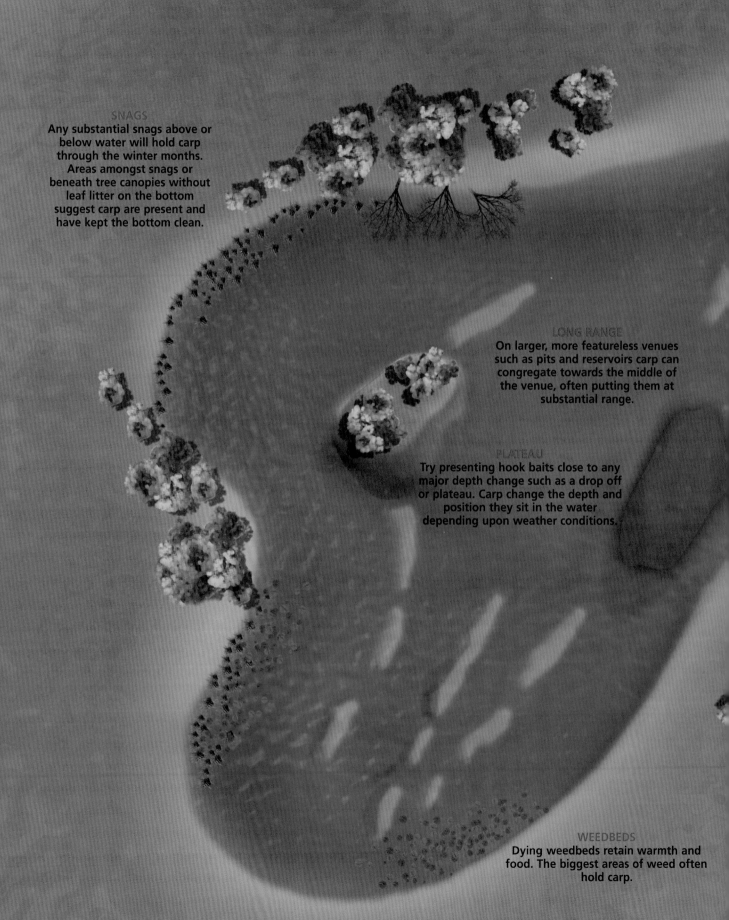

SNAGS
Any substantial snags above or below water will hold carp through the winter months. Areas amongst snags or beneath tree canopies without leaf litter on the bottom suggest carp are present and have kept the bottom clean.

LONG RANGE
On larger, more featureless venues such as pits and reservoirs carp can congregate towards the middle of the venue, often putting them at substantial range.

PLATEAU
Try presenting hook baits close to any major depth change such as a drop off or plateau. Carp change the depth and position they sit in the water depending upon weather conditions.

WEEDBEDS
Dying weedbeds retain warmth and food. The biggest areas of weed often hold carp.

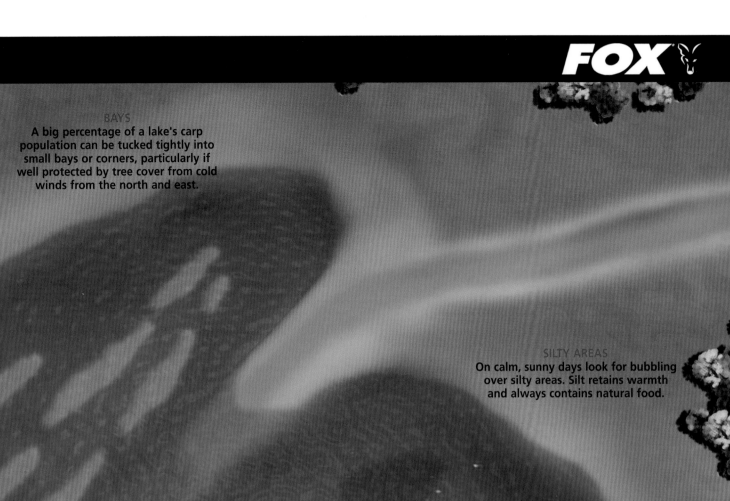

BAYS
A big percentage of a lake's carp population can be tucked tightly into small bays or corners, particularly if well protected by tree cover from cold winds from the north and east.

SILTY AREAS
On calm, sunny days look for bubbling over silty areas. Silt retains warmth and always contains natural food.

WIND DIRECTION
Carp often gather off the back off a cold wind where as the water is less chilled from being mixed with cool air.

AS temperatures drop carp are active for shorter periods during each 24 hour cycle and often become very localised and tightly clustered, factors such as temperature, air pressure, dissolved oxygen, light levels and natural food availability and more all combining to encourage carp to be more or less active.

Accurate location becomes even more important than at any other time of year, and there can be long periods where huge areas of a lake are completely devoid of fish. In the most extreme conditions carp have an incredible ability to find stable, protected surroundings in places we do not even realise they can get to. Experienced fishery management teams will recall countless stories of finding almost a whole lake's carp population tucked into small undercuts hollowed

out beneath the bank or along island margins in places we could never find them let alone fish for them.

Careful observation is the best way of tracking down winter carp. Even when almost completely inactive they will periodically roll or head and shoulder, particularly at dawn and dusk - similar to us having a stretch and a scratch when stirring after a period of slumbering.

Between November and March if you see one carp show it is highly unlikely it is on its own. Casting baits anywhere where you see definite signs of carp is a very big step to catching winter carp. If a hook bait is close to even sluggish carp there is a good chance it will be taken at a time of the day or night the carp become more active.

WEATHER WATCHING

SPEND time watching big carp in a pond and it becomes easy to see how strongly the weather patterns dictate behaviour. Dropping air temperatures and cold winds from the north and east that chill the water or high air pressure bringing cold nights and hard frosts will see carp become almost motionless, conserving vital energy. Although they will sometimes stir slightly and re-arrange their position when in the company of other fish there can be periods of several days when carp barely move and eat nothing.

In contrast, big weather fronts moving across the country from the south or west bringing milder air, rain and big winds can quickly switch carp back on, seeing them become incredibly active for short periods. These big changes in weather - with air temperatures rising and sometimes even reaching double figures in Centigrade - can bring bumper catches to those who are braving the winds and rain.

A lake that has appeared lifeless for several weeks can turn on with carp crashing and showing everywhere.

Carp can be caught in the cruellest weather and regular baiting and intense campaign style fishing can bring steady winter results for the dedicated but changing weather remains the single biggest factor affecting winter carp behaviour. Paying close attention to the weather forecast allows you to pick conditions, hopefully timing visits to coincide with the best chance of action.

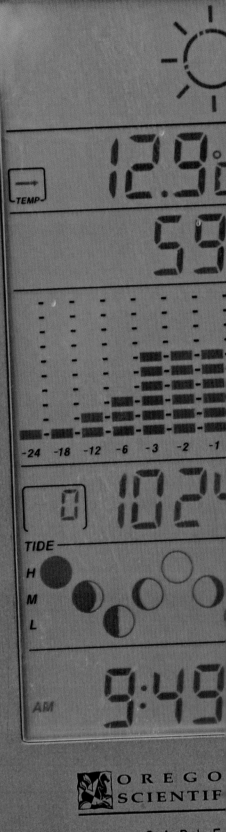

ONE AT A TIME TRAPS

WINTER carp are not looking to feed hard, and relying on small amounts of bait brings more consistent results. In the warmer months we may encourage several or even dozens of carp to feed hard but that is much more difficult to achieve between November and March.

Regular bait introduction makes catching winter carp much more straight forward, a handful of free offerings made available in the same few spots every day or couple of days is the perfect way to wean carp on to your bait.

It doesn't take long for carp to become very tuned in to your bait and begin to look for it, improving catches dramatically. But the travelling, time and expense puts such an approach beyond most carpers, and trying to feed more heavily less regularly is not as effective and encourages bird life to feed on your bait rather than carp.

If you can't feed areas regularly or are only fishing occasional trips rather than regular sessions it's wiser to be cautious with free offerings. As always, once you've introduced bait you can't take it out. Single, highly flavoured hook baits, dipped baits and small PVA

bags and stringers are more than enough to stimulate carp to feed without risking over feeding. On venues that are being regularly fished there's a steady introduction of bait from lots of anglers that helps keep carp nosing around for food without you needing to worry about prebaiting.

Carp can be convinced to eat substantial amounts in cold weather, but heavy baiting is best left to those with time to fish long sessions and take advantage of more aggressive tactics. Good location and fishing for one carp at a time puts you in with the best chance of regular action.

COLD WATER BAITS

DEDICATED big carp anglers have long debated successful cold water baits. Historically it was suggested boilies with the highest nutritional value ingredients scored best, others arguing in favour of lower food value baits that are more easily digested and quickly pass through a fish. Today, commercially ready rolled baits account for most of the boilie market with their key ingredients known only to the manufacturers, but word very quickly spreads about successful recipes. Internet forums, magazines and even on the bank discussions will help guide you towards proven winter boilies. Bait companies themselves will also guide your choices through catalogues and websites. It's widely agreed that boilies with a high fishmeal content tend not to perform well in cold water - typically dark brown or deep red in colouration. Softer frozen ready-mades score well, particularly fruity baits like pineapple, tutti frutti or plum, although plenty of savoury baits also perform consistently well. Whichever you choose, smaller 10-15mm baits tend to score more reliably in cold water than larger 18-22mm baits.

More significant than boilie choice has been the demise in popularity of boilies altogether as a winter carp bait in recent seasons. As the carp bait industry has developed and techniques have advanced the role boilies play in winter carp fishing has diminished.
With so many effective methods that rely on alternative hook baits there has been a swing away from introducing any number of boilies as free offerings and it is entirely possible to fish a winter through and catch dozens or even hundreds of carp without needing any boilies at all. Instead, many experienced carpers would opt for single pop-ups or bunches of maggots every time.

"Many experienced anglers are now opting for bunches of maggots rather than boilies"

PELLETS

Marine and trout pellets lose some of their effectiveness in cold water and are best avoided, their high oil content preventing them leaking attractors so readily. Fast breakdown compressed pellets are a better choice, often available from bait companies with added attractors to match successful boilie recipes. Hemp pellets are also excellent.

MAGGOTS

A live, moving bait maggots stimulate the most sluggish carp. Productive fished as a bunch on maggot clips with small PVA bags of grubs, maggots are also one of the few baits that can be fed very heavily, very successfully in cold water. Although pricey, a gallon in a swim can bring a tremendous feeding response and multiple catches even in bitter conditions.

MAIZE AND CORN

Sweetcorn continues to catch carp all year, is highly visible and easily digested. If feeding corn, harder maize or artificial corn are the best choice on the hair to prevent nuisance fish stripping bait off.

HEMP AND PIGEON MIX

Although considered warm water baits both hemp and pigeon mix are outstanding winter feeds, digested easily in the lowest temperatures. Ideally suited to session fishing, the small seeds keep fish of all species browsing for long periods, ensuring bait remains in a swim even when diving birds are problematic.

MEAT

Enjoying a revival in popularity, especially when twinned with PVA sticks of meaty groundbait, a small section of Peperami or cube of luncheon meat can also score well. Use Fox luncheon meat props to keep softer meats safely on the hair.

HIGH ATTRACT POP-UPS

A RECENT development, highly visual pop-ups with massively increased levels of attractors have had a massive impact on winter carp sport.

Pop-ups made with many times the usual recommended flavour dose and twinned with high levels of dye produces baits that are both highly visible to carp from long distances away and offer a huge level of attraction, providing a hugely boosted stimulus for a carp to come and investigate and eat the hook bait. Fished in isolation or with small PVA bags of pellets and dips high attract pop-ups are devastating.

Most major manufacturers provide a range of boosted, high attract pop-ups with proven flavour and attractor packages. So effective are they that you could arguably fish a whole winter through never introducing any free offerings, relying purely on the pull of high attract pop-ups to catch good numbers of carp.

Look for baits with bright, rich colours that don't fade in water with good levels of smell, buoyancy and a spongy, needle friendly texture for easy mounting on a rig. Some combinations of flavours and colours consistently prove themselves to be outstanding catchers. Carp seem to have an incredible fascination with yellow baits, and yellow pineapple pop-ups produce time and time again even on difficult venues. Despite the universal faith in yellow baits white pop-ups are the most visible of all underwater, and are outstanding catchers especially with proven flavours like chocolate, squid or cream.

On different days and on different venues carp can show a distinct preference for one type of hook bait, making it wise to carry several colours and flavours of pop-ups. The Evolution glug case is supplied with six tough screw top tubs for convenient storage of different hook baits and dips.

Each jar carries a label to remind you which one is pineapple and which one is scopex, ensuring you never forget which one is catching!

TOP TIP
SMALLER hook baits are more effective in the winter. Try trimming the edges off 15mm pop-ups to make them smaller and provide a faster leak off of attractors.

DIPS

MAGNIFYING the attraction from a hook bait dozens or hundreds of times over without increasing the number of free offerings, dips score best in colder water, helping carp locate hook baits more easily and providing extra stimulation to feed.

Typically thick, sticky liquids dips stick to the surface of baits and end tackles, boosting the pull in the immediate area of the rig. Available from all major bait manufacturers they vary from dips that contain little more than dye and flavour to blends of highly potent food extracts that match successful boilie recipes. As a rule darker dips tend to contain attractive food ingredients rather than just carrying dye and flavour and are more effective.

Most dips are based on solvents such as sugars and contain no water, allowing them to be used with PVA without it beginning to dissolve. Dunking a complete rig and cobweb PVA bag or stringer prior to the cast traps enough dip for your rig to smell as attractive as dozens if not hundreds of free offerings on the lake bed, yet the only food present is on the hair or around the hook bait - massively increasing your chances of a take. Lead core leaders and leads can also be dipped, and diluted down dips added to spods to boost attraction in a swim without adding numbers of free offerings.

Many commercially available dips are not supplied in user friendly jars, bottles or pots, making it difficult to dip PVA bags and rigs and running a risk of breakage or leaking. Leaking dips are not just messy but can ruin clothing, tackle or expensive camera equipment stored nearby. Fox Glug Pots have a rubber sealed screw top preventing dips leaking and contain a draining plastic cage retainer that clips on to the side of the pot, allowing baits to be removed easily for rebaiting rather than chased around a dip with fingers and needles.

DIPS are not designed for baits to be immersed for long periods. Hook baits should be dipped either immediately before casting or left in the dip for a few minutes to half an hour to coat them and boost their smell. Leaving boilies or pop-ups in dips for longer periods draws moisture out of them, leaving them rock hard and often requiring a drill to mount them on a rig. Such bullet hard baits will not release attractors or work as effectively as hook baits with their softer, original texture.

BEATING THE BIRDS

FOOD is scarce for all animals not just fish when winter sets in. It doesn't take long for bird species to learn to exploit anglers baits as a valuable additional food during this lean time of the calendar. Birds such as coots and tufted ducks diving and picking up free offerings and hook baits can be hugely frustrating, especially after it has taken a long time to position hook baits accurately.

Carp can be caught unexpectedly from amongst the worst bird activity in a swim, but more often it ruins your chances of action and is enough to demoralise the hardiest of carpers. Seagulls are also very adept at stealing boilies as they hit the surface of a lake from a catapult or throwing stick. Don't be deceived - every bait they go for they get, often leaving little or no free offerings reaching the bottom. On some venues simply picking up a catapult is enough for keen eyed seagulls to begin circling in anticipation of a free meal at the expense of the carp.

Darker baits are less readily spotted by diving birds and small mass baits like hemp and mixed particle are impossible for them to pick up, as are finely crumbled boilies, fast breakdown pellets and groundbaits, ensuring there is always food present in a swim to interest a carp.

Regular recasting with small PVA bags and dipped baits is a great way of building the level of attraction and numbers of free offerings in a swim without any tangible baiting up to draw attention to your hook baits.

Other than at dawn and dusk catapults and throwing sticks become impractical and spods are the only way to guarantee safe introduction of free offerings.

If you're fishing a venue regularly, baiting spots at dusk or after dark gives carp a valuable 12-14 hours head start finding free offerings before the onslaught of diving birds begins again the following morning - making free offerings introduced

at the end of a day session more likely to be found by carp than those introduced in daylight. Try this if birdlife is hampering your chances of carp settling over your feed.

REGISTERING EVERY INTEREST

TAKES from winter carp will not always be spool spinning one noters. Fast takes are still common but sluggish fish in cold water are equally likely to gently tighten or shake the rod tip and slowly pull a bobbin up to the rod blank.

Fox EOS and high specification Micron alarms feature variable sensitivity, allowing the smallest interest at the end tackle to be accurately registered at the rods. Using single bank sticks for each rod and pointing the rod tip directly at the hook bait reduces line friction and the resistance of the rod tip, Swingers or Hangers set with minimum counter balance weights to prevent false indications from undertow and wind also improving how effectively you register small pulls.

Illusion fluorocarbon main line, as well as being less visible than standard monofilament lines also features significantly less stretch, improving the responsiveness of your indication system.

FEEDING TIMES

AS water temperatures tumble carp become much less active and need to feed less as their energy requirements drop. Unlike during the warmer months when carp are active and can often be persuaded to feed at any time of day or night when temperatures are low they will feed for very short periods. These feeding spells can become very regimented, and at times it can be possible to virtually set the clock by their feeding habits.

Keeping an eye out for patterns in capture times can help you plan shorter visits of just a few hours to coincide with these hot spells.

Day sessions can be very productive, with any sunshine and small increase in oxygenation and warmth spurring carp to become more active but late afternoon through to midnight is often a key time for catching carp from autumn through to Christmas, with an hour or two either side of dusk a very reliable period. By the time we're into the New Year daylight action is often on the increase again.

COLD COMFORT

WITH cold winds and low air temperatures a crucial part of winter carp fishing is bearing the elements whilst still fishing effectively with regular hot food and drinks helping maintain your core body temperature.

Any shortcomings in your bivvy, sleeping kit, clothing or footwear will quickly see you become uncomfortable and lose enthusiasm.

Generously sized for the biggest anglers Evo 5 Extreme and Evo 5 sleeping bags use DuPont Qualofil and synthetic hollow fibre fillings with polar fleece linings for maximum heat retention. Both models secure to bedchairs and feature heavy duty crash zips on both sides for a quick exit at any time.

Sleeping bag covers like the Zzz thermal cover and Zzz Sleepeeze add a second layer of insulation and prevent your sleeping bag becoming damp, fitting to a bedchair with Velcro loops.

A second skin on a tent or shelter improves insulation and reduces condensation. Most Fox shelters have the option of a dedicated winter skin. Alternatively pick a twin skin design tent like the Easy Dome series. Groundsheets insulate against cold rising from beneath your shelter.

Softer ground and unsettled weather make it more important to root tents and shelters down firmly. Fox threaded pegs and Euro Bankstick storm poles secure all bivvies from being uprooted by gusting winds.

Quality thermal and waterproof clothing keeps you warm and dry outside the bivvy. Thick socks and a thermal hat are standard issue but a neck warmer like the Fox fleece version improves comfort dramatically.

When nights draw in at 4-5pm avoid going to bed early then being wide awake in the small hours. Halo Bivvy Lights provide enough light to cook, read or tie rigs without the dangers of gas or petrol. A small radio also helps pass a few hours when the nights draw in early.

The Halo Elite Bivvy Light sticks to the inner of your shelter with a magnetic plate and is activated by EOS-R alarm heads, illuminating the bivvy for a fast, safe exit as soon as your alarms sound. Sensitivity settings allow you to choose from a single bleep to a full blown run to trigger the light, with variable illumination times before switching itself off.

Long nights and foul weather can make it easy to miss small indications from the rods. Remote sounders such as the RX-3 twinned with EOS-R alarms or auxiliary TXR transmitter and receiver unit that connects through the jack plug sockets of other Fox alarms ensure you hear every bleep.

CHAPTER 12

RIG PRINCIPLES

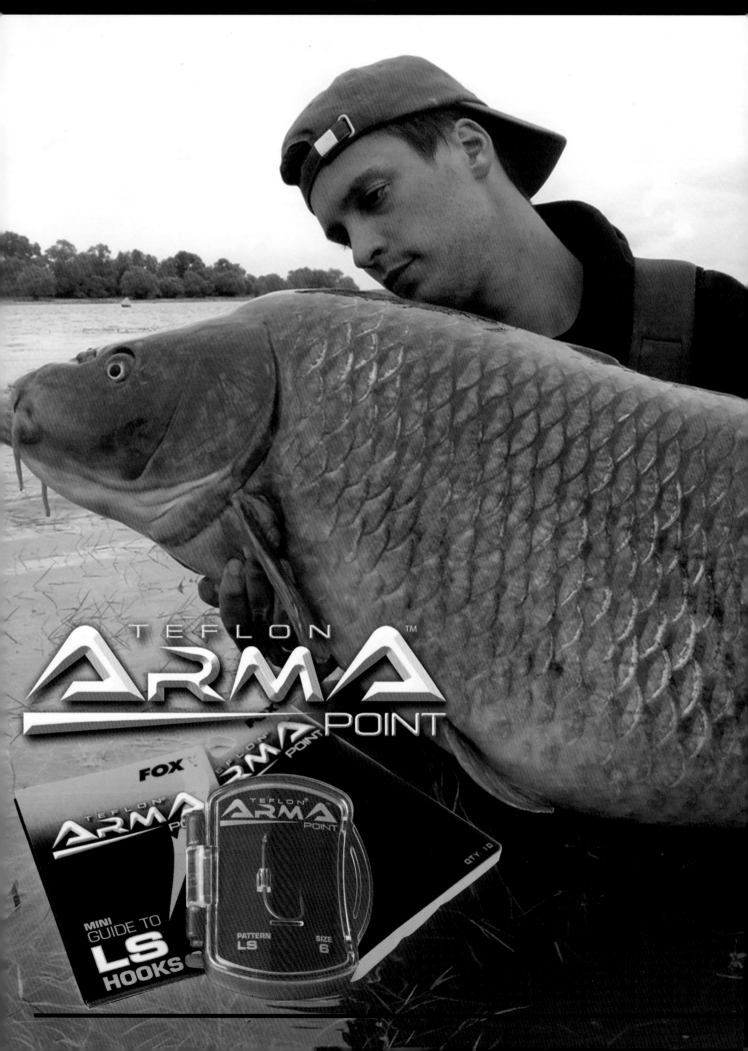

WHAT TO LOOK FOR IN A HOOK

TEFLON COATED
The long lasting non-reflective, non-rust Teflon coating improves rig concealment and ensures effortless penetration.

MACRO BARB
All patterns are available barbed and barbless. Barbed Arma Points feature ultra durable perfectly proportioned macro barbs to ensure solid hook holds and prevent hook rotation.

EYE
Eyes on all Arma Point patterns are perfectly formed with 100% closure to prevent any danger of hook length slippage or damage to lighter breaking strain materials.

ARMA POINT HOOKS
STAY SHARPER, LONGER

HOOKS that are razor sharp and stay razor sharp are the biggest single improvement most carp anglers can make to their rigs. The most mechanically efficient presentations, attractive baits and accurate rig placement mean nothing if your hook fails to perform.

How effectively a hook penetrates at the critical moment when a carp tightens a hook length determines how many carp you catch. A hook that fails to penetrate easily or that has become dulled by contact with gravel or from a previous capture is easily shaken out by a well practised carp. Razor sharp hooks that hold their points penetrate further, leading to more takes and fish on the bank, not missed opportunities.

Two years in development the Fox Arma Point range of hooks are probably the most technologically advanced specialist hooks available. Using a new high tech tempering process radically increases strength and sharpness resulting in super strong hooks with 'sticky sharp' and incredibly durable points.

Arma Points retain their razor sharp points when other patterns have become blunted or dulled, ensuring your rigs are always providing optimum hooking efficiency and converting pick ups to takes. During lengthy field testing one angler was able to use the same hook for more than 35 captures.

THE ARMA POINT RANGE
WHICH PATTERN?

CONFUSED by the number of hook patterns available? Subtle variations in shank length and shape, bend and point configuration result in changed mechanics and altered hooking properties making different patterns more suitable for different jobs. The Arma Point range offers unrivalled strength and hooking power with every possible presentation, bait choice and in every angling situation the modern carp angler might meet.

SSBP

SHORT SHANK BEAKED POINT

Incredibly versatile all-rounders the SSBP series suit bottom bait rigs for boilie and particle fishing, particularly over harsh gravel bottoms where the inturned point is less readily damaged. The short shank and wide gape also lends the SSBP to pop-up, snowman and even zig rig applications, helping to push the point up underneath the bait for fast hooking.

LS

LONG SHANK

The classic long shank pattern the LS is primarily a bottom bait pattern, lending itself to fast hooking with knotless knots, line aligners and angled shrink tube extensions. The shank length allows improved travel of hook baits on sliding rings and hairs for outstanding anti-eject performance. The point of the LS is marginally inclined to the shank to increase grip.

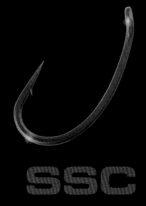

SSC

SHORT SHANK CURVED

An aggressive short shank curved pattern the SSC boasts incredible strength and turns quickly for solid hook holds making it the perfect choice for big fish amongst weed or snags when the pressure is on. Angled shrink tube extensions with the SSC result in some of the most secure hook holds possible, whether with bottom baits, snowman rigs, pop-ups or particle hook baits.

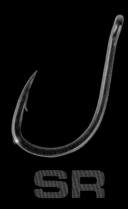

SR

STIFF RIG

Purpose designed for stiff link pop-up presentations the angled shank and slightly out turned eye sits the SR aggressively underneath pop-up hook baits and ensures high diameter stiff rig materials don't reduce the gape and impede hooking. A pattern that doesn't take shrink tube extensions well, the SR pattern performs best straight from the packet, lending itself to D loop presentations with fluorocarbon and heavy mono as well as pure stiff rigs.

LSC

LONG SHANK CURVED

Improving the renowned hooking properties of the original Fox Series 5 hook with Arma Point strength, durability and camouflage the LSC turns quickly, the curved shank shape making it very difficult for carp to eject. Suiting pop-ups, balanced boilie and particle rigs as well as the popular 360 degree presentation the LSC is a tremendous asset when tackling rig shy carp.

SSSP

SHORT SHANK STRAIGHT POINT

A classic all-rounder for all but the most heavy duty work the SSSP is at home with boilies and pellets on the bottom as with floating hook baits on the surface or zig rigs in the upper layers. The smaller sizes retain tremendous strength making them excellent choices for small hook baits and delicate presentations with maize, mini boilies and artificials. Where long shank hooks are banned long curved shrink tube extensions to larger sizes of SSSP hooks achieve the same aggressive hooking and anti-eject properties.

BARBED OR BARBLESS?

OPINION varies over the suitability of barbed and barbless patterns for hard fighting carp. Arma Points are available in both barbed and barbless, allowing the same efficient needle sharp patterns to be used whatever fishery rules dictate. Barbed Arma Points feature a precise macro barb, just large enough to prevent excessive turning of the hook during the fight, but still allowing easy unhooking.

BOXING CLEVER

ALL Arma Points are supplied in tough flip boxes that fit precisely into Fox tackle boxes, clearly displaying the size and pattern for efficient rig construction.

Each box features a high density foam insert, preventing hooks rattling and protecting points from dulling through hard contact with other hooks.

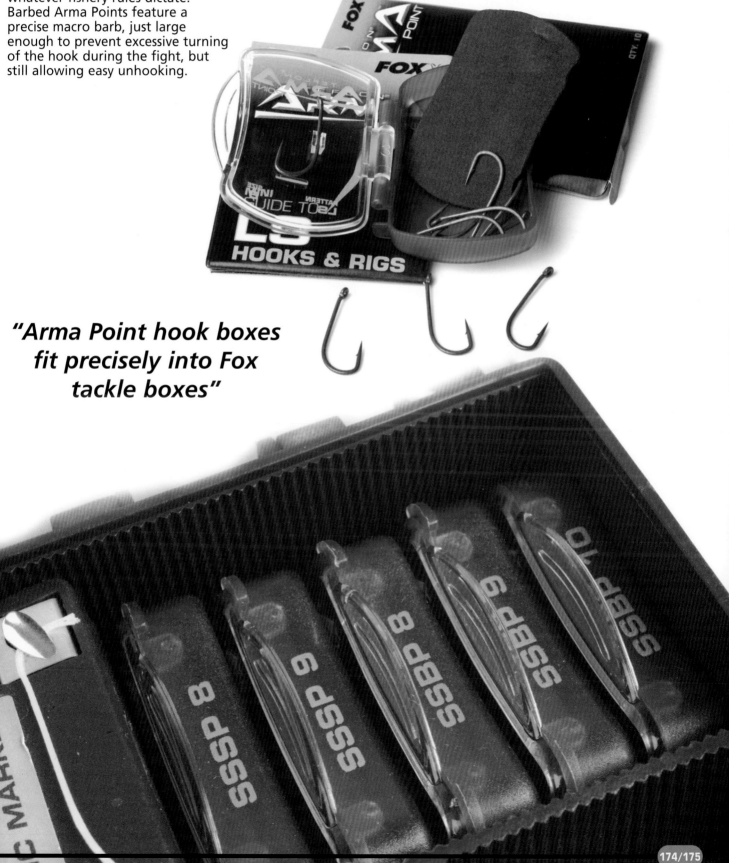

"Arma Point hook boxes fit precisely into Fox tackle boxes"

HOOK MECHANICS

EVER wondered what's the reason behind the long lengths of tubing in different shapes that extend hooks on popular carp rigs? Understanding rig mechanics helps us construct more efficient rigs that hook more carp and result in fewer losses.

Because chances of hooking carp are relative to the time spent on the bank much of carp angling revolves around self-hooking rigs rather than reacting to bites and actively striking hooks into fish.

Carp have incredible capacity to learn by association, far in excess of that shown by other species. Back in the 80s when carp anglers began to understand the apparent ease with which carp could eject rigs or shake partially set hooks out a rig revolution began with anglers developing all manner of end tackle adaptations to overcome problems of carp spitting hook baits out without being caught.

Ways of making hooks and hook baits more difficult to eject is a constant battle ground between thinking anglers and tackle conscious carp who have developed behaviours like head shaking to prevent themselves being hooked.

Although historically much rig theory is based on flawed or armchair thinking, there have been several key advances in rig mechanics that have contributed to today's effective self-hooking rigs, the two most important being the Line-Aligner and Knotless Knot.

1. *The Line-Aligner needs to be fished with a supple hook length to allow the hook to turn freely. Here we're using 15 lb gravelly brown Coretex, but braids like Reflex also work well.*

4. *Cut a 10mm length of 1.2-0.4mm Fox Shrink Tube and push a lip close baiting needle through the side wall of the tube 3mm from the end.*

THE LINE-ALIGNER

INNOVATED by carp and specimen ace Jim Gibbinson the Line-Aligner Rig of the 80s single handedly altered the way we construct carp rigs, bringing the benefits of good mechanics to the fore.

Jim realised that if the hook length exited the hook inside the line of the shank rather than being tied to the eye, when the hook length was tightened the hook turned aggressively point downwards to take hold.

Relate the changed rig mechanics to a carp that picks your hook bait up and then moves its head looking for another bait. As soon as the hook length is tightened the Line-Aligner rig turns and takes hold - often resulting in a panicked carp and a run. For bottom bait rigs the Line-Aligner still takes some beating. Here's how to tie it.

THE LINE-ALIGNER

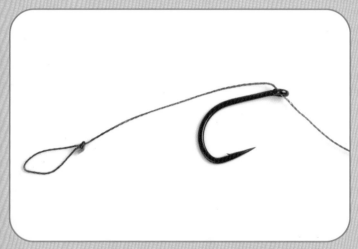

2. *Strip back 10cm of the coating of the Coretex then tie an overhand loop and set the hair length. We're using a size 6 Arma Point SSSP for a bottom bait presentation with boilies.*

3. *Whip a knotless knot and pass the tag end down through the eye. The knotless knot is explained on P179.*

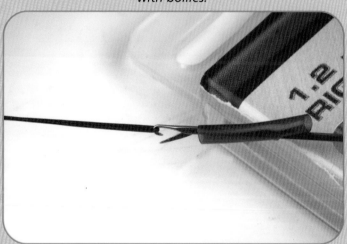

5. *Push the needle through the tube, pick up the hook length in the needle and pull the Coretex back through the shrink tube.*

6. *Slide the tube down the hook length and over the eye so the tube sits on the hook shank opposite the point and the Coretex is exiting the tube inside the shank.*

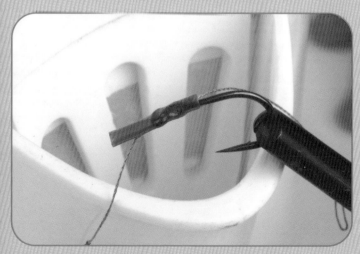

7. *Gripping the hook in forceps hold the hook and tube over the steam from a boiling kettle.*

8. *After you've seen the tube shrink down tight over the eye and hook shank remove the hook and tube from the steam and blow on it to cool and harden the tube.*

THE KNOTLESS KNOT

THE most widely used carp and specialist rig of all the Knotless Knot is a whipping rather than a knot and offers an easy and neat way to tie almost any hook length material with a precisely determined hair and effective hooking mechanics in seconds.

Like the Line-Aligner the Knotless Knot offers effective rig mechanics because the hook length material passes down through the eye of the hook, changing the angle of pull to inside the line of the shank. It helps a Knotless Knotted hook turn and take hold when a hook length is tightened or is pulled across the lips of a carp.

HAIR EXIT POINTS

THE Line-Aligner and Knotless Knot can easily be tied to vary the position the hair exits the shank.

With bottom baits a hair that exits the shank directly opposite the point has proven to be the most consistent catcher. It ensures the hook is taken in to the carp's mouth bend first, improving the chances of finding a hold.

Sliding hairs or hairs that exit on the bend or close to the hook are a feature of more complex anti-eject rigs designed to allow hooks to turn freely and are covered in Advanced Rigs.

"The Knotless Knot offers an easy and neat way to tie almost any hook length material with a precisely determined hair"

TOP TIP

A COMMON mistake is to feed the hook length up through the eye at the end of tying the knotless knot. Always ensure the line is passed down through the eye towards the point or hooking efficiency is reduced.

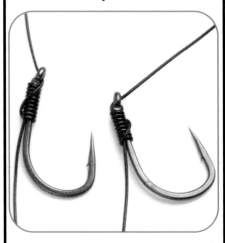

THE KNOTLESS KNOT

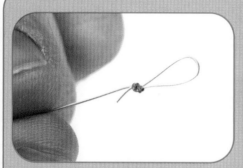

1. Tie a small overhand loop in the end of your chosen hook length material. It can be braid, mono, fluorocarbon or a combi-link material.

2. Thread your chosen hook baits on to the hook length material and insert the hair stop. Here we're using two 14mm boilies.

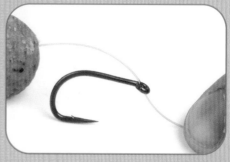

3. Pass the hook length down through the eye of your hook - here a size 6 Arma Point SSSP.

4. Keep passing the hook length down through the eye until the baits are sitting 10-20mm away from the bend of the hook.

5. Grip the bend of the hook and the hair to stop the baits slipping out of position and pull the hook length material down at right angles to the eye and shank.

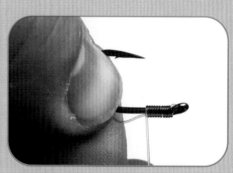

6. Whip the hook length towards you and then up and around the shank above the eye.

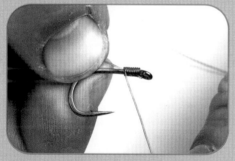

7. Keep whipping the hook length around the shank until you reach opposite the point of the hook. Ensure the coils of your hook length material sit tightly together without crossing over each other.

8. Grip the shank and the whippings to keep them in position and feed the end of the hook length down through the eye, exiting the same side as the point.

9. Pull the hook length tight to complete the knot.

SIMPLE SOLUTIONS

BOTH the Knotless Knot and the Line-Aligner are basic, yet highly effective presentations. Between them they have probably accounted for more carp in the last 10-15 years than all other presentations put together. The Knotless Knot is a more modern solution giving the same hooking advantages as the Line-Aligner. The fact that the Knotless Knot requires no additional tubing or access to kettle and steam makes it even more popular than the Line-Aligner, and

has become a standard presentation for bream, tench, barbel and chub specialists, as well as match anglers fishing commercial pools. The Line-Aligner is arguably slightly more efficient thanks to the shrink tube extension but there is little to choose between them.

Mechanically efficient rigs, both will hook a big percentage of carp that pick up a hook bait and move their heads looking for another bait.

With good location skills, attractive bait and careful application of free offerings they are all we need to

catch carp even on very difficult waters.

You might be surprised how many top anglers use rigs as simple as the Knotless Knot and Line-Aligner for virtually all of their fishing. Key Fox employee Andy little has seen most of carp angling's rig developments come and go in the last 30 years and now rarely uses anything other than a Knotless Knot, relying on keen observation, location skills and good bait application with a simple, efficient end tackle to catch carp everywhere.

THE HAIR

THE development of the hair rig by Kevin Maddocks and the late Lenny Middleton back in the early 80s shaped the way we fish for carp. No other single change to presentation since has ever made such a colossal difference to numbers of carp caught.

Angling thinking had always been that hooks needed to be buried in baits for the best chance of success. The principle of the hair rig was to mount the hook bait on a couple of inches of very fine 1-2 lb line tied to the hook.

The hook being detached from the bait was a revelation. Carp were unable to detect the line the bait was mounted on. Without the weight or feel of the hook directly associated with it the bait on the hair behaved like a free offering and was readily accepted.

Used with hard boilies and particle baits as soon as the bait was confidently taken the hook followed the bait into the mouth

and was free to catch hold rather than needing to be struck through a direct hooked bait.

The hair used with the first heavy lead bolt rigs changed expectations and success rates overnight. People suddenly caught more carp in one day or night than they had in the whole of the previous season.

The hair has never been improved and the principles behind its success remain unchanged. Today, virtually all carp rigs involve baits mounted on a hair rig, but the original principle of the hair has been lost and is widely misunderstood.

HAIR BASICS
BOTTOM BAIT PRESENTATIONS

USING bottom baits the biggest single improvement you can make to your rig is to use a longer hair and increase separation between the hook and the bait.

Hairs have gradually become shorter and shorter. Look carefully at most carp rigs in common use and there is very little clearance between the base of the bait on the hair and the bend of the hook. Hairs this short with little or no separation between the hook and the bait have simply become a convenient method of attaching baits.

To benefit from the original principles of the hair rig we need to increase the hair length. Within reason the greater the distance between the hook and the bait the more fish you catch.

For many anglers there is a huge mental block to overcome in lengthening a hair. The fear is that a carp will pick the hook bait up but not get the hook in its mouth. But by lengthening the hair you are more likely to get the hook into a carp's mouth because the hook bait is taken more confidently.

Remember, the carp wants the food item that you have threaded on the hair. It smells and tastes good. What he doesn't want is a hook. Carp are more than clever enough to relate the feel of something hard, sharp and metallic with danger when they pick a piece of food up - it happens every time they get caught. If a carp feels something suspicious closely associated with a piece of food it eats, the food is ejected in an instant. Because most rigs have the hook and the bait so close together we make it easy for carp to feel the hook almost instantly and get rid of it.

If you increase the length of the hair, the hook bait can be picked up without a carp feeling the hook or the weight of the hook. With no immediate suggestion that something is attached to the bait a carp happily takes the bait followed by the hook into the mouth.

Longer hairs also work to your benefit once inside the mouth. The greater the separation between hook and hook bait the more freely the hook drops to the floor of the mouth to find a hold as the link tightens. If a carp ejects a hook bait fished on a long hair the increased distance between the bait and hook prevents the force of ejection being so directly applied to the hook, increasing its chances of staying in the mouth or finding a hold on the way out.

HOW LONG?

THERE'S no right answer as to how long to fish a hair on bottom bait rigs. Where most hairs have only a few millimetres clearance between hook and bait, increasing hairs to leave around 20-25mm from base of the bait to the bend of the hook will produce an instant upturn in results and numbers of carp hooked.

Carp of 20, 30 and 40 lb have very big mouths and hairs can realistically be made as long as 40-50mm with outstanding results, although with smaller single-figure and double-figure carp hairs this long may cause problems with hooking outside the lips.

Don't assume that long hairs can't be fished with shorter links - the advantages of the long hair remain the same. Even with links as short as

15cm a hair length of 20-25mm provides improved presentation and rock solid hook holds.

One of the most noticeable effects of long hairs is the increase in action you receive from all species, not just carp. Using longer hairs you'll find you catch more bream, tench and even roach, a sure sign that your presentation is improved and your hooking efficiency has improved. If you lack the confidence to change hair length this much in one go, gradually increase it over several sessions, 5-10mm at a time. Very quickly, you'll be a convert and your hairs will become longer than you ever imagined.

BEATING TANGLES

ONE irritating side effect of lengthening hairs on bottom bait rigs is their tendency to wrap around the hook shank during the cast. Even minor tangles hit confidence hard and reduce the efficiency of a rig, sometimes to the point where it will catch nothing. When using longer hairs lick a nugget of High Riser dissolving foam and squeeze it around the hook shank, trapping the hair in position through the cast. The foam

quickly dissolves and pops to the surface directly above the rig leaving you with perfect presentation every time.

POP-UP RIGS

IN contrast to bottom bait rigs, pop-up rigs almost exclusively work more effectively with a shorter hair.

When baits are suspended off the bottom hooking is much faster than with bottom bait rigs. As soon as a hook bait passes over the bottom lip an effective pop-up rig has the opportunity to hook a carp if the hook is positioned correctly.

There is no advantage separating hook and bait in this situation, it is more important to ensure the hook is sitting aggressively under the hook bait with the point ready to prick a carp as soon as the bait is taken.

Most successful pop-up presentations use short hairs or sliding ring D loops exiting just above the eye. This bait mounting effectively pushes the hook upwards relative to the bait to make it hard for carp to mouth the hook bait without getting hooked.

TYING HAIRS AND BAIT MOUNTING

HAIR LOOPS: STRUGGLING to tie a neat, secure hair loop in the end of your hook length before whipping Knotless Knots? Here's how...

1. Double 6-7cm of hook length material back on itself. Running wet fingers along it helps keep the doubled length of line as one.

2. Hold the beginning of the doubled length of line between your right finger and thumb and the end of the loop in your left finger and thumb.

3. Turn the end of the doubled line clockwise and trap the line in your right finger and thumb.

4. Now push the end of the doubled line through the loop you have formed.

5. When tightening down push the knot towards the end of the hair to reduce the size of the hair loop.

6. Trim the tag end and you've got a secure, neat hair loop to retain boilie stops or pellet pegs.

RIG TOOLS

NEAT rig construction and bait mounting requires the correct tools. Here's a guide to what you'll need in your tackle box or bait bucket.

DRILLS

Essential for hard baits a 1.5mm drill helps mount nuts, floating pet biscuits or air dried boilies. The new fine 1mm Fox Pellet Drill makes drilling marine and trout pellets much easier, the finer diameter splitting baits much less readily and allowing pellets as small as 4mm to be mounted on hair rigs.

BRAID BLADES

Ever struggled to trim hook length materials neatly? Using scissors for day to day jobs like chopping down hook baits or removing rig bits from packaging will damage the blades and make them ineffective when cutting braid and combi-link materials. Fox Titanium Braid Blades are purpose designed for cutting hook length materials slicing cleanly through the toughest link materials, but to keep them performing at their best use them only for this job.

NEEDLES

A selection of different needles caters for different baits and presentations. The Fine Hook Baiting Needle has a small recess rather than a sharp barb so as not to damage delicate and small hook baits and reduce damage to braided hairs. The Lip Close variant accommodates larger diameter hair materials, the latch that closes over the hook preventing damage to baits as they slide on to the hair.

A Stringer Needle is longer than baiting needles, allowing numbers of baits to be transferred to a stringer in one movement preventing multiple loadings of a needle to construct one stringer. The large hooked end securely holds PVA tape or string.

KNOT LOK RIG GLUE PEN

Superglue is notorious for leaking or being impractical to use after a couple of trips with the cap glued on or the nozzle jammed. The Knot Lok Glue Pen dispenses a drop of glue at a time, and features an anti-clog nozzle to continue dispensing small amounts of waterproof glue to secure knots or mount baits.

TENSION BAR

A multi-use tool the Tension Bar is pushed through loops of booms on stiff link presentations to ensure they remain straight. With two diameter bars the tool also tightens loops and hook knots or even picks fiddly rig bits from storage boxes.

TYING SLIDING HAIRS

SOME more advanced presentations covered use sliding hairs tied to metal rig rings to improve rig mechanics, helping to allow hooks to turn freely and take hold and allow the bait to move along the shank if the rig is ejected. Presentations featuring sliding rings encourage anglers to tie baits direct to them. With bottom baits this reduces a rig's effectiveness because it reduces the hair length to zero. It also reduces flexibility, preventing double baits, or combinations of baits to be used as more than a single boilie can't easily be tied on. Tying a hair to a sliding ring that can be threaded through baits as usual allows you to increase the separation between hook and bait for increased action and vary the hook bait you are offering beyond a single round bait.

1. Take a 7-8cm length of fine braid or bait floss and pass it through the sliding rig ring.

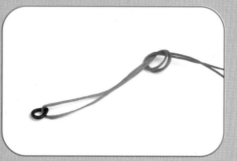

2. Ensuring the line is doubled and wetted to keep it together tie an overhand loop in it.

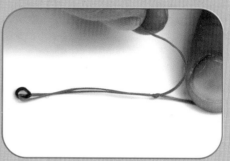

3. Tighten the loop down, wet with saliva then pull the tag ends to shorten the looped section down to whatever length you want the finished hair.

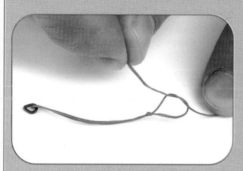

4. Tie a granny knot with the two tag ends, tightening them down on to the overhand loop.

5. Tie a second granny knot then snip the tag ends down to around 2-3mm.

6. Carefully offer a lighter to the tag ends to blob them down and prevent the looped hair slipping open.

7. Slide the hair over the shank of your chosen hook and follow it with a sliding rig stop.

8. Thread baits on as usual, keeping the overhand loop at the end of the hair where the stop is inserted.

9. Fox Hair Widgets offer a neat way of adjusting the position a hair exits the hook.

RIG PRINCIPLES

UNDERSTANDING the basics behind good presentation will catch far more carp than copying advanced, fashionable rigs.

If you had the opportunity to inspect the end tackles and rigs on the rods of today's most successful carpers it might be a surprise how simple they are. With the free exchange of information and ideas in books, magazines and on the internet there are very few rig ideas that aren't widely shared and available to all.

Relying on simple, effective presentations like the Knotless Knot and Line-Aligner and paying attention to the basic aspects of your rigs and changing them is enough to catch you a tremendous number of carp from the trickiest waters.

LENGTH OF HOOK LENGTH
WITH so much reliance on self-hooking rigs the length of your hook length is crucial.

A huge percentage of hook lengths in use today are between 12cm and 20cm, and because carp routinely pick up baits attached to links of these lengths they become very adept at dealing with them.

It's not glamorous and doesn't involve sliding rings and complicated rig theory but shortening or lengthening your links is a highly effective way of catching more carp.

Very short links are in fashion, and it's easy to appreciate how a shorter hook length can be successful. As soon as a hook bait is picked up and passes over the bottom lip the hook length is straightened and the lead forces the hook point in resulting in a take.

Where 15 to 20cm links are commonly used shortening your links to 6-8cm can massively increase the number of takes you get. Carp get little or no leeway to manoeuvre, as soon as they pick a bait up it's all over and the hook is in.

Short links are successful in solid PVA bags and particularly when fishing over baited areas with small food items like pellets, hemp and spod mixes. They are excellent over hard bottoms but care needs to be taken with end tackle choice to present such short links effectively in silt or on weedier waters.

Longer hook lengths are much less popular, partly because it's harder to understand how a carp will hook itself if you give it a lot of freedom to move a hook bait around without encountering the resistance of a lead. But with the carp world at large going shorter and shorter longer links are probably more effective than ever.

Lengthening them is the other way of changing the behaviour of the hook bait outside the parameters a carp generally encounters. With hook lengths of 30-50cm the hook bait is much less obviously attached to a fixed point of resistance when it is picked up. It's as crude in principle as giving carp enough rope to hang themselves, but can be a productive tactic even for very difficult carp. Longer links also make it much harder for carp to shake hooks out when they take hold - they can't use the weight of the lead so readily because it isn't so close to the hook.

Long links work excellently with larger feed items like boilies and large pellets and big particle baits like tiger nuts, especially when used with a light scattering of free offerings, stringers of PVA bags rather than tight, heavily baited areas. Unlike short links, long hook lengths tend to offer good presentation over almost any bottom including gravel, silt and light weed.

HAIR LENGTH
ALTHOUGH pop-up presentations work best with very short hairs, varying the length of hairs on bottom bait rigs is enough to get buzzers sounding where they have previously been silent.

Most rigs have little clearance between hook and base of the bait, but the longer the hair the more carp you catch.

Experiment with longer hairs on productive waters, you will see an increase in action straight away. Hook holds are improved and losses reduced. With bottom baits the only time to avoid long hairs is when using short 6-8cm links which can make it difficult for carp to get the hook into the mouth before the hook length tightens. Lengthening the hair by 20-30mm is a simple improvement that will bring more carp than many of today's so called advanced rigs.

LEAD SIZE AND ARRANGEMENT

THERE are so many end tackle options from in-line leads to running rigs and helicopter rigs that we can often increase our catch rate by changing the size and mounting of a lead.

In the same way that hook lengths tend to be a similar length across most rigs lead sizes are also typically between 2 and 3 oz.
The popularity of leads this size isn't so much related to hooking efficiency, more that standard issue carp rods of 2.75 lb and 3 lb balance well with these size leads and cast them easily and accurately.

For ease it's best to categorise end tackles as semi-fixed or running and using either light leads or heavy leads. Making a change to one of these aspects of your lead arrangement can make a big difference to results.

Most carpers use semi-fixed leads, but running rigs offer improved indication and make it much harder for carp to shake hooks out when they make a mistake and pick a hook bait up.

Changing to lighter or heavier leads that are commonly in use is also a great tactic. Lighter 0.75 oz to 1.5 oz leads plop in rather than crashing in to the water, spooking carp less and nagging hooks in without carp feeling the huge jolt of a bigger lead when the hook length tightens.

Equally, where 3 oz leads are as heavy as the carp routinely see, a much bigger 5 oz lead might drive a hook home harder and panic a fish that is quite used to dealing with hooks pulled in from 2-3 oz versions. Such heavy leads don't cast well but for close range or margin work can be a big edge.

HOOK SIZE

HOW big are your hooks? Reducing the size of the hook you use can bring extra action. Basic angling principles apply equally to big carp as roach and perch. The finer your tackle the more bites you get. Dropping from a size 16 to a 20 when maggot fishing results in more bites. Size 8s catch more carp than size 4s.

Even in size 8s, 9s and 10s, hooks like the Arma Point range are tremendously strong and able to cope with big fish amongst snags and thick weed. The smaller, and more importantly lighter, the hooks you use the less easy it is for carp to detect them - a bit like the difference between finding a large or small bone in a fillet of fish. A big bone you detect straight away, a smaller one might take a couple of chews.

HOOK BAITS AND FREE OFFERINGS

BAIT application and rigs are always interlinked. If carp are keen to eat something they will get caught on virtually any rig no matter how crude - witness carp that get caught on wire traces, trebles and deadbaits by pike anglers in the winter.

The more enthusiastically carp feed the easier they are to catch. The first reaction to blanking is often to change rigs, but application of bait looks at the problem from another direction.

The same carp that isn't fooled by a knotless knot and 30 boilies might feed harder and be caught on the same rig if you fed two kilos of freebies. The same rig that isn't catching with boilies might bring multiple catches with maggots on the hair. Switching to mini boilies can be enough to go from blanking to catching.

Carp are fickle creatures and different quantities and types of free offerings or different hook baits make huge differences in how hard they feed and how readily they get caught. Finding baiting situations or hook baits that flick their switch makes complex rigs unnecessary. If a carp is feeding hard enough it will always pull a hook into itself using the simplest end tackle.

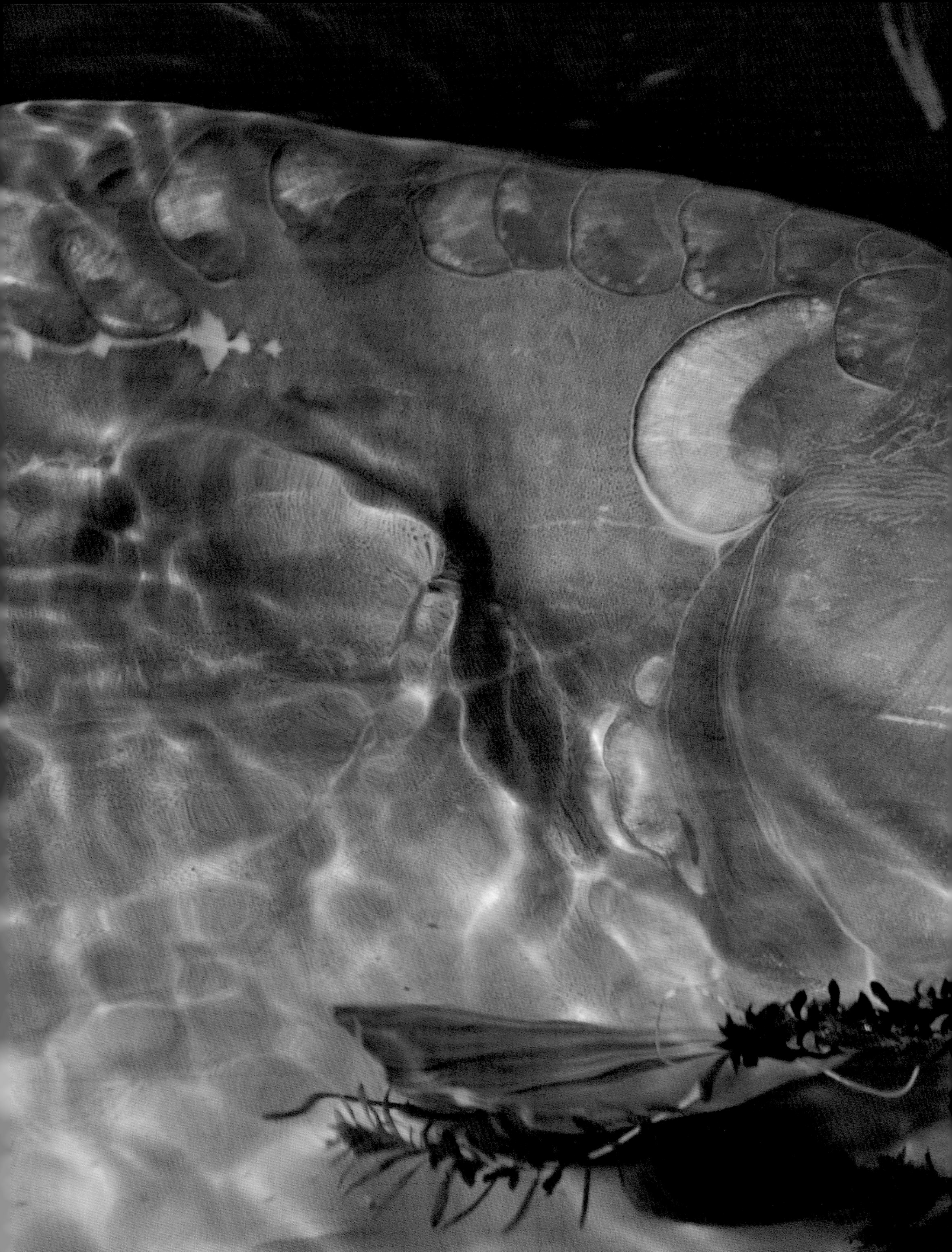

KEEP IT SIMPLE

PAYING attention to lead size and mounting, length of hook length, hair length and hook size gives substantial potential to vary your presentation enormously without having to tie complex rigs.

Rigs are only a very small aspect of successful big carp fishing. With accurate location, attractive bait and thoughtful bait application rigs become much less critical.

Sharp hooks and mechanically efficient end tackles are all we need to catch consistently. Experienced, successful anglers don't rush out to try the latest most fashionable hooking arrangements, instead considering the components and properties of simple rigs and altering them along with bait application and hook bait choice to find a successful combination.

- Good location is the most important factor to get right to catch carp consistently.

- Even a poor rig in the right place catches more than a complex rig fished nowhere near carp.

- The harder carp are feeding on your bait the less important rigs become.

- Before you alter rigs, experiment with different types and quantities of feed.

- Varying the size, shape and type of hook bait you offer can make more difference than rig changes.

- Use different length hook lengths, lead sizes, hooks and hairs on each rod to see which works most effectively.

CHAPTER 13

ADVANCED RIGS

AS CARP become more heavily pressurised being caught becomes a constant danger. If not avoiding clumsy and poorly disguised end tackles and hook baits completely, they become very well practised at picking up hook baits and ejecting them with ease. Watch margin feeding carp in clear water and it will amaze and perhaps demoralise you how effortlessly rigs are picked up and ejected without any apparent concern. If you could hook all the carp that ever picked up your hook bait you would very quickly catch all the carp you ever wanted.

Because carp angling relies on self-hooking principles rather than actively striking there has been constant experimentation from some of carp angling's most fertile minds to try and catch carp out more readily and improve the numbers of pick ups converted to takes and hooked carp.

SO WHAT EXACTLY IS AN ADVANCED RIG?

Studying the mechanics of a rig, including the behaviour of the hook, the characteristics of the hook length material and lead arrangement and how they behave together when a hook bait is picked up and passed over a carp's bottom lip can improve the effectiveness of our rigs.

There is no ultimate rig on offer, only developments of sound, proven principles that improve upon the mechanics and hooking capabilities of more standard presentations.

With so many variables involved hooking and landing carp it is always difficult to say how crucial rig developments are to success.

There's no question that simple, effective rigs in the right places will always catch more than advanced rigs fished in the wrong spots, and that moving swims or experimenting with hook baits and bait application are often more crucial to success than more complex hooking arrangements. But with the sheer pressure carp on many fisheries are under, simple changes and improvements to the way your rigs perform can result in a significant increase in action.

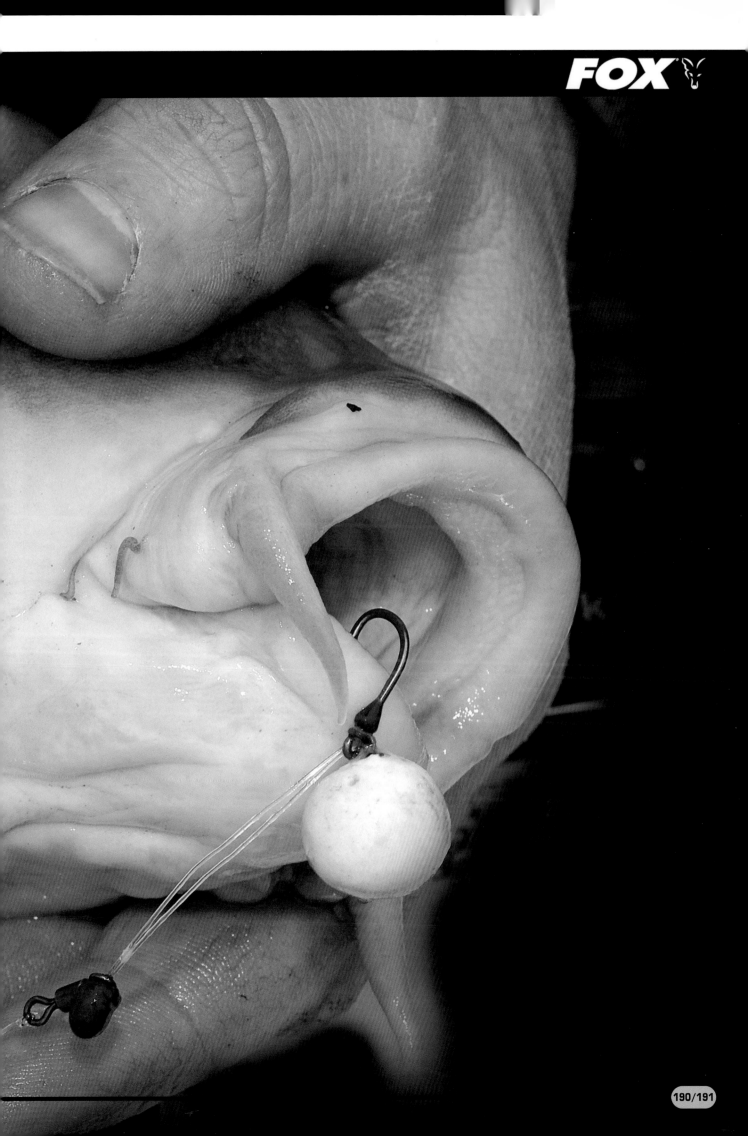

CORETEX COMBI LINK

A SUPPLE low diameter braid coated with a camouflaged semi-stiff outer, Coretex is one of the most versatile hook length materials of all. Tied as a combi-link Coretex is probably the single most reliable presentation you can take to any carp venue in the UK and possibly the world. It is the go anywhere, catch a carp presentation that comes first off the rig board for several members of the Fox Carp Team.

Leaving the semi-stiff coating intact for the majority of the hook length provides tremendous anti-tangle and improved anti-eject properties, a supple hinge improving the turning characteristics of the hook. Twinned with the short shank, aggressive and incredibly strong Arma Point SSC it will cope with the toughest situations around weed or snags but still offers subtle presentation.

IAN CHILLCOTT
"This is the rig I have used almost exclusively over the last 12 months, with either a bottom bait or a snowman hook bait.

I first put this rig through its paces at the famous Rainbow Lake in France, coinciding with testing of the new Arma Point hooks.
Lots of big fish came my way including my best at over 60 lb on the size 6 SSCs. If ever there was a lake to

test things on this is it and I can't see me changing the hooks I use or the rig in the immediate future. I have used the rig in five different venues, each completely different and it has never let me down.

For a long time I felt that the longer shrink tubing extensions used to create a safe bent hook effect were way too long, this rig uses a much shorter hook extension which makes it turn more quickly, putting the hook in the right position to take hold sooner than any other rig I have used."

The only change is the length of the hook length depending on the make up of the bottom
I'm presenting a hook bait over. Over gravel it is kept short at 5 - 7 inches (12-20cm) and lengthened to 8 - 12 inches (20-30cm) when fishing over short weed or in silt.

Using the kwik change swivel allows links to be changed in seconds with fresh baits already threaded on and balanced if required. Because links are so quickly changed it helps ensure you are always fishing with the sharpest hooks, and waste no time re-rigging."

Countless fish in excess of 30 lb have fallen to this rig, including a lifetime's ambition for Chilly, a pedigree English common of 44 lb 4 oz

THE CORETEX COMBI LINK

HOW TO TIE THE COMBI LINK

1. Strip back 5-6 inches (12-15cm) of outer coating from the Coretex.

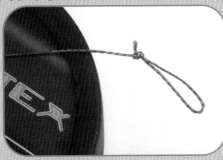

2. Tie a small overhand loop at the end of the exposed braid to form the hair and trim the tag ends.

3. Thread the hook bait on the hair before whipping the hook on to ensure the hair is set the correct length. Here we're using a 14mm boilie with a single grain of yellow plastic corn on top.

4. Thread the unstripped end of the Coretex down through the eye of a Size 8 Arma Point SSC.

5. Trap the hair between finger and thumb along the shank so the distance from the base of the bait to the bend of the hook is 5mm.

6. Whip an eight to ten turn knotless knot up the shank of the hook, passing the unstripped end back down through the eye to tighten it down.

7. To aid the turning of the hook further add a 10mm length of 1.2-0.8mm shrink tube, sliding it up the shank to completely cover the knotless knot.

8. Hold the hook in forceps and steam over the spout of a boiling kettle.

9. As soon as the tube shrinks remove it from the steam and pull the hook length so the tube sits at 90 degrees to the point. Blowing on the tube cools and sets it to retain its position.

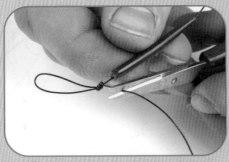

10. Thread an anti-tangle sleeve down the hook length then tie a figure of eight knot in the end of the hook length.

11. The end tackle is a safety lead clip on the end of a lead core leader using a kwik change swivel. The hook length is slipped into the hook on the swivel and the anti-tangle sleeve pushed over it to secure it.

12. Alternatively by tying a ring swivel to the hook length the Coretex combi link can be fished with any lead arrangement of your choice.

SLIDING JOINTED STIFF LINK

A DEVELOPMENT of the popular jointed stiff link presentation the sliding jointed stiff link is a pop-up rig that offers an extra dimension of movement, improving hooking characteristics and making it a very difficult rig for carp to shake out.

The stiff boom kicks the bait away from the lead and lead core and the ability of the upright hooking section to slide through and freely spin around the swivel that connects it to the boom section makes the rig incredibly aggressive, searching for a hook hold once it is picked up. Despite the stiff nature of the boom and hooking section the rig boasts almost complete freedom of movement in any direction.

Fox Rigidity is the ideal material for stiff presentations, with excellent anti-eject properties but knotting easily for accurate rig construction, and combines with the Arma Point SR hooks that feature a slightly out turned eye for improved hooking with high diameter stiff materials.

A tremendous presentation for big fish on pressurised venues the sliding jointed stiff link improves stiff presentations right through from ease of construction to freedom of movement for the hook bait.

TOP TIP
BLOBBING the tag ends of knots with a lighter improves knot reliability when using stiff links. Using a lighter with an adjustable flame turn it down to a minimum then slowly offer the flame towards the tag end until you see the heat from the flame melt the line into a blob. It will blob long before the flame gets close to touching the tag end. Always keep the rest of the hook length well away from the flame, and always blob knots inside a bivvy or indoors where wind can't catch the flame and cause damage to the line.

SHAUN McSPADDEN
"This rig is a clever way of achieving the same hooking characteristics as the 360 degree rig without using a long shank hook. Because there's less metal involved it's also a more subtle presentation and can be safely used for carp of any size.

It's so aerodynamic I use it for almost all my medium to long range fishing, and being stiff I've never had a single tangle even in heavy winds.

The sliding jointed stiff link can be fished with in line leads or lead clips over very clean bottoms, but it performs better with a helicopter rig that lays the hook length out as the lead core leader or anti-tangle tubing settle.

Sliding the back stop a foot up the lead core allows you to cast heavy leads long distances into silt and the hook length slides back up the leader and sits beautifully on top of the silt rather than being buried. Over gravel and hard bottoms shortening the distance between bomb and back stop down provides faster hooking but the movement of the hook length swivel up the leader prevents carp shaking their head and dislodging the hook point.

It's an ideal single hook bait rig, but over any quantity of free offerings shortening the boom section down to just 5-6cm also makes it devastating. The rig needs a very buoyant pop-up to perform best, Mainline's pineapple or Fruit-tella are favourites. If the weight of the bead and size 11 swivel doesn't sink the bait mould a small piece of Hi-SG putty around the bead at the bottom of the stiff upright section. Hook holds tend to be in the middle of the bottom lip so hook pulls are rare helping you land the vast majority of fish that you hook. Takes are normally fliers but at range add extra drag weights on Hangers to register drop backs effectively.

I've caught carp from every venue I've used the rig on including pressured day ticket venues, southern pits and silty meres. This goes to show the effectiveness of the Sliding Jointed Stiff Link."

THE SLIDING JOINTED STIFF LINK

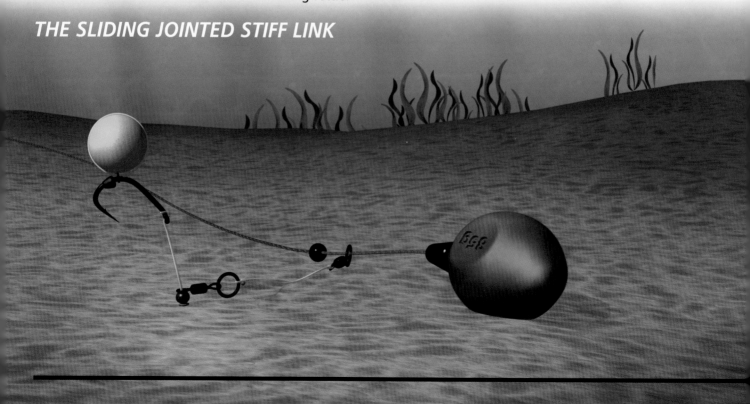

HOW TO TIE A SLIDING JOINTED STIFF LINK

1. Take an 8-10cm length of 15 lb Fox Rigidity and double it over, tying an overhand loop 2-3cm from the apex of the doubled line.

2. Snip off the tag ends to 2-3mm and gently blob them by offering a lighter towards them. The length of this finished loop plus the length of the hook dictates how far off bottom your bait will be presented.

3. Slide a tungsten bead - available from all good fly fishing shops - and a size 11 swivel over the doubled line to sit by the blobbed overhand knot then push the apex of the loop up through the eye of a size 7 Arma Point SR.

4. Pull the bend of the hook up through the middle of the parallel strands of Rigidity that are forming the loop.

5. Now pull the tungsten bead and swivel to tighten the Rigidity loop down around the eye of the hook.

6. Thread a rig ring on to the hook followed by a rig stop. Position the rig stop at the top of the shank at the beginning of the bend. Tie a 14-16mm braided hair to the rig ring.

7. Tie a fresh length of Rigidity to the other end of the swivel running along the upright hook section with a clinch knot, blobbing the end with a lighter for security.

8. Tie the other end to the eye (not the ring) of a ring swivel to create the finished boom section, again blobbing the knot for security. Aim to tie the boom to 8-10cm.

9. Cut an 18" (45cm) length of camo lead core and splice a speed link at one end and a spliced loop at the other.

10. Thread a knot protector bead, followed by the ring of the ring swivel on your hook length, a camo flexi bead and a 1.5cm length of rig silicone.

11. Remove a swivel from a distance pear lead with wire cutters and clip it on the speed link, pushing the knot protector bead over the link. Different size and shape leads can be switched in seconds and quickly removed to carry rods made up.

12. Push the camo flexi bead over the silicone and position it up the lead core to act as a back stop. Over gravel leave 8-12cm between the lead and back stop. Over silt the back stop can be fished as much as 30cm back up the lead core.

THE MAG-ALIGNER

MAGGOTS are an incredibly productive big carp bait that can bring huge catches in short periods. Their effectiveness has been more widely appreciated with the increase in venues containing numbers of big carp with few other nuisance fish.

There are numbers of ways of fishing maggots, from using bunches of grubs as an alternative hook bait when PVA bagging to introducing a gallon or more at a time to induce competitive feeding in numbers of fish. One of the most effective maggot tactics has been the Mag-Aligner presentation developed by experienced carper and author Rob Maylin.

The Mag-Aligner is a complete one carp trap that uses a PVA bag to concentrate a huge number of maggots around the hook bait with no other free offerings in the swim. Careful observation showed that presenting maggots in such a tight fashion resulted in carp exhibiting an almost predatory response - wolfing down the ball of writhing maggots with one gulp and flare of their gill plates.

Such a clump of maggots also offers a visual target that carp spot from long distances, and perhaps also hear with so many maggots wriggling together.

A small maggot hook bait presented next to the maggots from the bag is taken in at the same time as the thousands of free maggots - resulting in hooked carp every time.

Results on the Mag-Aligner have been devastating, Rob's own catches including huge numbers of 20s and 30s to over 40 lb from tough southern pits in just short day sessions. The Mag-Aligner is a tactic in its own right as much as an advanced rig.

THE MAG-ALIGNER IN USE

IN use the Mag-Aligner is not a delicate method. With a 2-3 oz lead and a large bag of maggots tied to it the casting weight becomes 4-6 oz. Such a load requires powerful 3.25 or 3.5 lb test rods, and it is a short to medium range tactic not one that can be used to present baits at range. Reels must be spooled with 15 lb or preferably 18 lb mono to prevent crack offs.

1. Take a 2-3 oz in-line lead and trim off the soft rubber insert where it exits the rear of the lead.

5. Cut a 20cm length of Coretex combi link. Strip back 6-7cm of the outer coating and tie on a size 10 Arma Point LS, leaving 1-2cm of exposed braid beneath the eye.

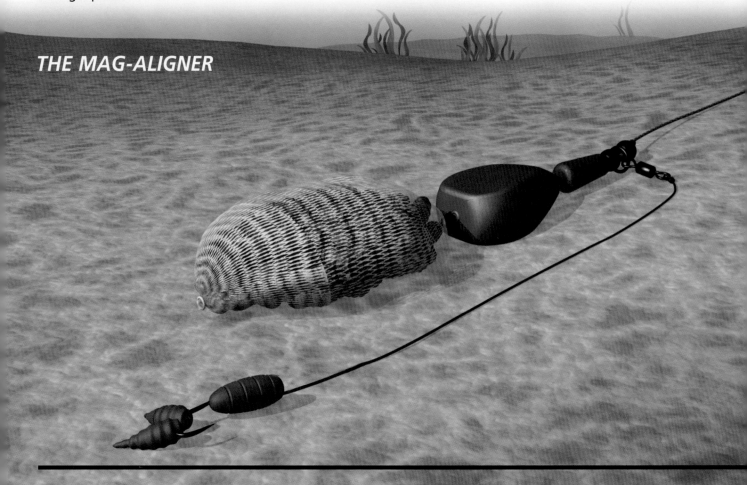

THE MAG-ALIGNER

HOW TO TIE THE MAG-ALIGNER

2. Thread the lead on to a ready spliced lead core leader and ring swivel.

3. Thread on a camo flexi bead followed by a ring swivel threaded through the ring, a second camo flexi bead and a 1.5cm length of 0.5mm rig silicone.

4. Twist the top camo flexi bead over the rig silicone and slide it down to sit 1-2cm above the top of the lead.

6. Push the point of a splicing needle in through the side of a soft rubber maggot and then through along the centre to exit at the narrow end. Match the colour of the rubber maggot to the colour of the real maggots you will be using.

7. Pull the unstripped end of the Coretex back through the rubber maggot.

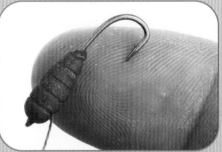

8. Moisten the maggot then slide it down the hook length and over the eye of the hook. This gives it the hooking characteristics of the line-aligner rig using an artificial maggot instead of shrink tube.

9. Tie the hook length to the ring swivel trapped helicopter style on the lead core above the lead. It should be 8-12cm.

10. There is no hair used for the Mag-Aligner. Thread two maggots on to the bend of the size 10 LS hook. Where allowed barbed hooks are preferable.

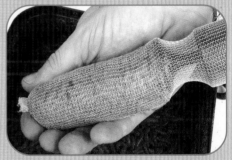

11. Two thirds fill a Network Micromesh funnel with maggots. Using the plunger compress the maggots hard and push them out of the tube to form a bag.

12. Tie the bag off tightly with an overhand knot and snip the bag off leaving an 8-10cm tag end.

13. Pass the tag end through the ring of the swivel in the nose of the in-line lead and tie it off tight to the lead with a couple of overhand knots.

14. Straighten the hook length to run parallel to the bag and lightly nick the hook point through the PVA mesh ensuring the point is facing out of the bag and not masked by a maggot.

When such a package of lead and PVA bag is cast out the disturbance is substantial. However, similar to fishing the Method feeder the deeper splosh of the Mag-Aligner hitting the surface appears to unsettle carp much less than standard end tackles being cast around, possibly because the noise more closely resembles a big carp crashing. In practice the

Mag-Aligner is an instant tactic and takes can come very quickly after casting out so be ready for some pretty hectic action. Fished amongst feeding carp it will often bring action in minutes rather than hours, and works most effectively when recast at signs of feeding carp. It's a great method for anglers that are prepared to put in lots of effort.

Watch carefully and don't be afraid to recast with another big bag of maggots if you see bubbling, coloured water and carp showing elsewhere.

Because the PVA bag uses a large quantity of maggots you can expect to use several pints even during a day session, each fresh cast or fish caught depleting your bait stock further.

Look to take between four and eight pints of maggots per trip. It's expensive compared with other tactics but the reward can be the fishing of a lifetime if you use the Mag-Aligner before it has been exploited on a venue. Surely that's worth spending a few extra pounds on bait?!

The Mag-Aligner has some limitations. It's best avoided on waters containing numbers of nuisance fish as it catches bream and tench every bit as effectively as carp. And it's not as effective on weedy waters as the maggots can soon crawl out of a carp's view.

But there are more venues where the tactic is outstanding than those where it is less effective, and it is devastating all year round, being one of the highest impact tactics innovated in recent seasons. It's definitely a tactic worth trying throughout the season!

SOLID PVA BAG RIG

PVA bags remain one of the greatest carp tactics yet devised, catching carp everywhere. But their widespread use is a double edged sword - carp know a small pile of pellets or other baits means an easy food reward but it often contains a potential danger from a hook bait.

Carp hoover up the free pellets without getting caught far more than most carpers realise. A few bleeps quickly after casting or a shake of the bobbin can often mean the contents of the PVA bag gone and no carp caught. On well stocked venues if a PVA bag hasn't produced a carp within the first 30 minutes you've often missed a chance and are advised to recast a fresh bag.

Solid PVA bags allow the lead and entire rig to be stuffed inside the bag with the pellets, making tangles impossible and allowing baits to be presented with confidence even in weed. Braided hook lengths are perfect for tucking rigs into bags. Reflex braid is super supple, sinks without additional weight and has an effective camouflaged finish.

Because PVA bags concentrate bait in a tiny area carp pick up the contents of bags with very little movement of their head and simple adaptations to a rig and end tackle maximise the chances of hooking fish.

COLIN DAVIDSON

"This is my standard bag rig and can be used on any venue over any bottom - it's a deadly go anywhere, catch a carp presentation. As soon as the hook bait is lifted up off bottom the hook point is under tension and instantly banged into a carp's mouth.

A carp only has to suck the hook bait over the lip and it's nailed but the supple Reflex braid ensures there's always enough play in the hook length for the bait to be taken in for a secure hook hold. Dumpy in-line leads concentrate weight at the nose where the hook length is tightened to for improved bolt effect.

Because the feed baits in PVA bags are usually small and lightweight like pellets and chopped boilies it's important to keep the hook and hook bait small and light. Arma Point LS 10s are perfect, although for big fish in more demanding swims switch to an Arma Point SSC size 9 or 10.

Even on such short links kwik change weights along the hook length improve hooking, instantly tensioning the hook as soon as the bait is lifted off bottom. The elastic tensioning system that secures kwik change weights eliminates any risk of damaging the braided link.

It's popular to use very short hairs and silicone tube to exit them just above the point but I still find increased separation of 10-15mm between the bend and base of the hook bait improves results and gives better hook holds, even with links as short as 8-10cm.

The rest of the rig and end tackle is simplicity itself. There's no need for anti-tangle tubing, lead core or any sort of leader behind the lead because with PVA bags you can't get tangles and the putty improves line concealment."

TYING A SOLID PVA BAG RIG

1. Thread a 2-3 oz in-line lead up the main line and tie on a ring swivel with a five turn grinner or Palomar knot.

2 . Two or three small blobs of Hi-SG putty moulded around the main line at 12-18 inch (30-45cm) intervals behind the lead help keep the main line pinned down for improved rig camouflage.

3. Tie an overhand loop at the end of a six inch (15cm) length of Reflex braid.

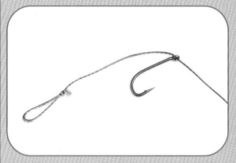

4. Pass the end of the Reflex down through the eye of a size 10 Arma Point LS, setting the hair length to 30mm from eye of hook to end of the hair loop.

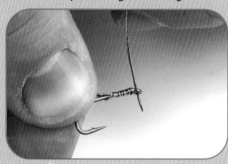

5. Whip a six turn knotless knot, passing the tag end down through the eye to complete the knot.

6. Cut an 8mm length of 1.2-0.8mm shrink tube and slide it down the hook length and over the hook to completely cover the whippings of the knotless knot.

7. Grip the hook with forceps and hold it over the steam from a boiling kettle. When you see the tube shrink down remove it from the steam.

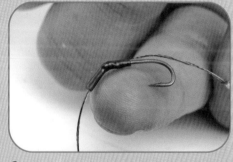

8. While the tube is still soft pull the hook length so it is at an angle of 45 degrees to the shank and blow on the tube to cool it and set it in this position.

9. Tie the end of the Reflex braid to the ring swivel in the nose of the lead using a five turn grinner knot. The link needs to be kept short at 7-10cm.

TOP TIP

TRY drilling and hair rigging 10 and 14mm halibut pellets to use as hook baits inside a solid PVA bag. A Fox 1mm pellet drill makes it easier to drill them without splitting and Fox pellet pegs keep them securely on the hair. When filling bags with pellets you get more bites with pellets rather than boilies on the hair.

10. Position two AAA kwik change pop-up weights together half way along the braid between the lead and the hook.

SHRINK TUBE BENT HOOK RIG

SHRINK tube hook extensions are a common feature of many of today's rigs, helping to improve hooking potential.

Hook extensions change the point of balance of a hook, encouraging it to turn to find a hold. The effect an extension has on hook mechanics is clearly seen when drawing hooks back along the palm of the hand. A long curved or angled tube extension causes a hook to turn point down and instantly take hold when tension is applied to the hook length. Liken this to the behaviour of your rig when the hook bait is taken into a carp's mouth and the hook length tightens to the lead. Such aggressive mechanics that encourage a hook to find a hold instantly can only lead to more hooked carp.

From the early 90s when the bent hook principle was first popularised it has been shown that curved rather than bent tube extensions provide optimum rig efficiency. Using Fox shrink tube to create the extension is more versatile than using long shanked hook patterns, offering a lighter finished presentation and allowing the rig to be used safely for carp of any size.

Consequently it works best with larger baits, the extra weight of the baits themselves helping achieve fast turning of the hook. It's at its best over baited areas of larger 14-20mm pellets or 14-20mm boilies, and particularly suits snowman presentations and double baits.

The rig stop at the top of the point guarantees the best chance of the hook taking an instant hold in a carp's mouth when the bait is taken in and the hook length is tightened, but it's a common mistake to have the baits tight to the bend of the hook. Leave at least 10mm between the bend of hook and base of the baits. On anything other than pop-up rigs increased hair length improves rig performance. The free movement of the hair back down around the bend and top of the shank allows the hook to stay in position fractionally longer even if a carp tries to eject the rig. Hook holds will all be in the bottom lip or the scissors.

Because the outer coating of Coretex is semi-stiff the rig is incredibly tangle proof, but the same length and shape hook extension and hair can also be used with braided hook lengths like Reflex or combi-links using Rigidity and Illusion boom sections and short braided hinges.

1. Cut a 30cm length of Coretex and strip back 8-10cm of the outer coating.

5. The finished hook should have the end of the shrink tube in line with the point. If the tube hasn't shrunk like this, steam it again, remove from the steam then tension it into the right position before blowing on it to cool and set it.

THE BENT HOOK IN USE

The principle of the bent hook extension can be applied to any hook, but in practice it works better with larger sizes, a bigger hook improving the anti-eject qualities and making the rig more difficult to get rid of once a carp has picked it up.

"A long curved or angled tube extension causes a hook to turn point down and instantly take hold"

HOW TO TIE A SHRINK TUBE BENT HOOK RIG

2. Tie the exposed braid to the eye of a size 6 Arma Point SSSP, leaving 2-3cm of exposed braid behind the eye.

3. Cut a 2cm length of 1.2-0.8mm shrink tube down the hook length, over the eye and 5mm down the shank.

4. Gripping the bend of the hook in forceps hold the hook and tube over steam from a boiling kettle. Without needing to be shaped or formed the tube should shrink down to form a gentle curve.

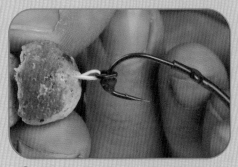

6 Tie a 30mm braided hair to a rig ring and slide the ring on the shank followed by a rubber rig stop positioned just above the top of the point.

7. Tie the tag end of the hook length to the ring of a ring swivel, leaving the finished link 15-20cm.

8. The shrink tube bent hook is incredibly versatile and can be fished with in-line leads, running rigs, safety clips or helicopter end tackles dependant upon the nature of the venue and the lake bed.

THE SHRINK TUBE BENT HOOK RIG

THE CHOD RIG

THE Chod Rig is the most aggressive presentation of modern times, an out and out mugging rig that hooks fish the instant a bait is picked up.

A pop-up only rig developed from the jointed stiff link the Chod Rig uses the same upright hook section as on a jointed stiff link but fished straight up direct from a lead core leader with no boom section.

As soon as a carp takes the bait over the lips it feels the full resistance of lifting the lead core leader, main line and indication system, tensioning the hook point straight in. Takes are explosive.

Fox 20 lb Rigidity is the perfect choice for Chod Rigs, the extra breaking strain absorbing the huge stresses on such a short link through a fight. Arma Point SR hooks are designed for use with such stiff hook length materials, the out turned eye allowing a hook bait to be presented perfectly D loop style in the correct position to sit the hook aggressively for fast hooking.

THE CHOD RIG IN USE

INCREDIBLY versatile the Chod Rig can be used on almost any venue at any time of year and in a variety of baiting situations - often with equally spectacular results.

Because the hook length is only a few inches long and revolves around the lead core leader the Chod Rig is a very long casting end tackle that simply cannot tangle. It's effective with single high attract pop-ups, especially in the winter and spring, but equally deadly over baited areas.

The few inches movement between the stop beads and silicone sleeves gives an extra dimension of movement, preventing carp shaking the rig out when they first lift off bottom having been hooked. The hook length fished back up the leader away from the lead also prevents the weight of the lead being used to bounce the hook out. Takes are either absolute ripping spool spinners or drop backs that look like your line has been cut with the bobbin falling on the floor. Extra drag weights on Hangers and Swingers help indicate drop backs more effectively.

Commonly fished at just 5-8cm off bottom the Chod Rig is as deadly over soft bottoms as hard gravel, as long as care is taken over the positioning of the top bead and tube back stop. Over soft bottoms it must be pulled further back up the leader to settle slowly down over silt rather than be pulled deep into it.

1. Cut an 18" (45cm) length of camo lead core and splice a speed link at one end and a spliced loop at the other.

5. The top length of tube and bead should be pushed three or four inches (8-10cm) further up the leader, acting as a back stop for the ring swivel.

The Chod Rig must be fished on a helicopter rig - much of its success due to the way tension is applied to the hook point. When a carp lifts the hook length it is subjected to steadily increasing tension from the lead core and main line not direct pressure from a lead.

THE CHOD RIG

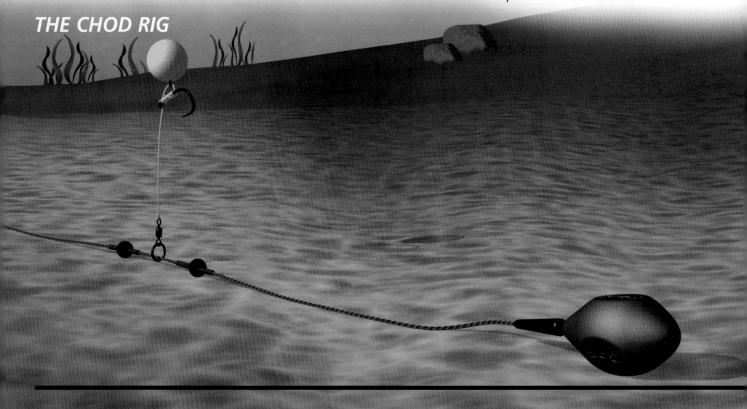

HOW TO TIE A CHOD RIG

2. Thread a knot protector bead, followed by a 1.5mm length of 0.5mm rig silicone, a camo flexi bead, the ring of a ring swivel then another camo flexi bead and 1.5cm length of rig silicone down the lead core.

3. Remove a swivel from a distance pear lead with wire cutters and clip it on the speed link, pushing the knot protector bead over the link. Slide the swivel, beads and silicone down to sit above the lead.

4. Push the camo flexi beads to sit over the ends of the silicone closest to the swivel. Moisten the tube with saliva and push the bottom bead and tube stop six inches (15cm) up from the lead.

6. Snip off a 20cm length of Rigidity 20 lb and pass it down through the eye of a size 7 Arma Point, leaving a 4-5cm tag end where you would normally have a hair.

7. Whip an eight turn knotless knot, passing the tag end down through the eye towards the point to tighten the knot down.

8. Thread a rig ring on the 'hair' length of Rigidity then snip the end to a sharp point with rig scissors before pushing it down through the eye to form a small D loop tight to the whippings of the knotless knot.

9. Gripping the hook between finger and thumb pull the hook length line tight so it is gripped parallel to the shank and knotless knot. Trim the tag end of the D loop within 3-4mm of the eye.

10. Keeping the hook length line trapped slowly offer a lighter towards the tag end of the D loop until you see it melt and form a small blob. Be very careful not to allow the flame to touch or damage the hook length line.

11. Withdraw the flame and after a few seconds for the line blob to cool, pull the D loop line so the blob butts up against the underside of the hook eye.

12. Tie the tag end of the hook length to the eye of the ring swivel using a once through the eye three turn blood knot, aiming to leave the complete link at 5-8cm maximum.

13. It's vital to take your time and lubricate the Rigidity with saliva when tightening down the blood knot so as not to kink the line. After the knot is tightened trim the tag end to 3-4mm and blob with a lighter for security.

14. Tie a pop-up on to the rig ring and the Chod Rig is ready to cast out. Over soft bottoms the sliding stops on the lead core leader should be pushed up the leader by as much as 12-15 inches (30-38cm) to allow the rig to settle on top of silt.

HELPING YOU CATCH MORE

Other books and DVDs in the Fox range...

 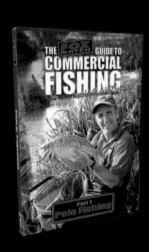  
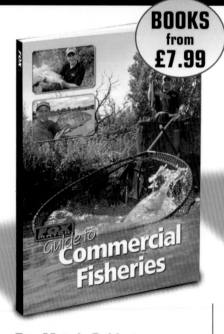  

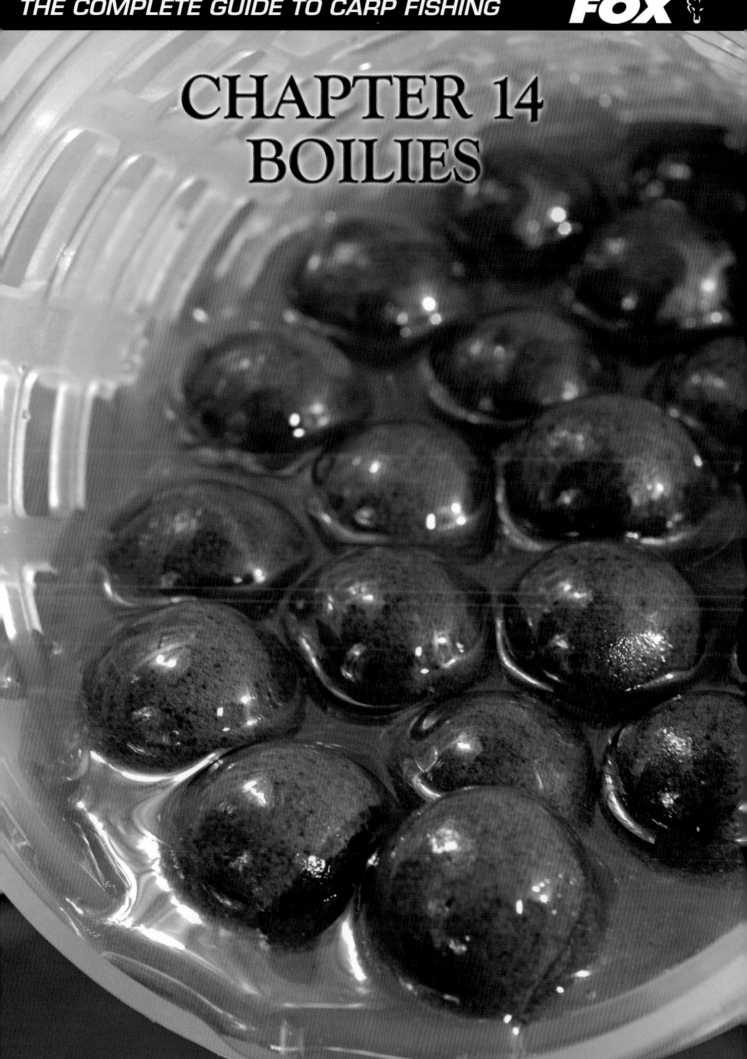

CHAPTER 14
BOILIES

BOILIES

BOILIES or boiled baits were a logical advancement from the paste baits that were a feature of early carp angling. To prevent smaller fish whittling away their soft, attractive pastes carpers hit on the idea of dropping them in boiling water to form a protective skin around the bait, and from there boilies were born.

Wheras baits like maggots, casters or worms can be eaten by almost any fish that swims, a ball of paste with a tough skin was only readily eaten by bigger fish, introducing a selectivity that allowed carp to be realistically targeted and caught by design without interference from other species.

From humble beginnings with experiments limited to mixing bowls in kitchens the carp bait industry is now a commercial giant, with the biggest companies boasting dedicated boilie production lines that borrow technology from the food industry to churn out hundreds or thousands of kilos of boilies every day in all manner of different colours, flavours and sizes. Investment in such advanced, high output machinery ensures the baits you pick up in your local tackle shop are perfectly round with the correct levels of attractors and manufactured to the exact same proven recipe each and every time you buy.

Twenty-five years ago the choice of baits for serious big carp anglers was limited to boilies or particle baits like hemp, corn and tiger nuts. In the last decade carp angling has become so popular and techniques have developed so widely that with the development of commercial feed pellets, ready prepared particles in tins and jars, groundbaits, artificial baits and ready-made hook baits like pop-ups and bottom baits in tubs, boilies straight out of the bag are only one of a huge number of baits in the modern carper's armoury. But the convenience they offer ensures they remain the most popular carp bait choice of all.

WHAT'S IN A BOILIE?

ALL successful boilies have one common ingredient - a little bit of mystery! There has been 30 years intense development of boilies and carp bait manufacture, and in that time you can be sure that almost any substance that can be ground down, liquidised, poured or measured and mixed with eggs has been included in a bait recipe somewhere.

From Marmite and Angel Delight to amino acid complexes, food concentrates and potent pharmaceutical extracts to high grade milk proteins and fishmeals shipped from the other side of the world there are any number of ingredients that can be part of a successful boilie mix.

In the past boilies could be quite easily categorised based on the balance of their constituent ingredients, either milk protein baits, birdfoods or fishmeals. Nowadays, with huge networks of contacts in the human food industry and pet and animal feed industries established bait firms have access to ingredients and expertise that are far beyond the boundaries of

the interested angler who wants to make bait in the kitchen, making it impossible to label baits so easily. Good, nutritious, attractive boilies are typically a varied blend of ingredients that may include fish, milk, vegetable or nut derived proteins, carbohydrates and energy sources.

When you buy bait from a reputable company you are taking advantage of years of experience devising and testing successful boilie mixes ensuring that you are literally buying confidence in a bag. Whether you know or understand any of the complexities of what a bait contains or how it is made is largely irrelevant - the acid test is how readily it catches carp.

FISH OR FRUIT?
ALL manner of additives can be used to improve the pull of a boilie, from essential oils to bulk food oils, powdered extracts and taste enhancers and powerful synthetic flavours. There are few rules in the world of carp bait, and the sheer variety of tastes and smells in popular boilie recipes makes it difficult to categorise baits or generalise about performance trends.

But in higher water temperatures of April through to October some of the most reliable and consistent boilies are baits containing high levels of fishmeal. Nutritious, salty, and packed with energy rich oils, fishmeals are regarded as one of the best carp bait additives of all time. Their only drawback is that in lower winter water temperatures the oil content of fishmeal based boilies makes them less easily digested and less able to release attractors that may stimulate a carp to feed. From October to March dark brown or deep red coloured rich fishmeal boilies are best avoided.

In contrast baits that depend upon fruity flavours and enhancers tend to perform more effectively in colder water. Flavours such as pineapple and tutti frutti dissipate readily even in near freezing water because of their chemical composition, helping pull carp effectively all year round. Often used in high carbohydrate boilie mixes they typically pass easily through a carp's gut all year round, ensuring they continue to perform year after year.

FROZEN OR SHELF-LIFE?
READY rolled boilies are either available fresh frozen or as shelf-life baits. Frozen baits are rolled, boiled and dried by the manufacturers then frozen whilst still fresh, and supplied to tackle shops to store in freezers until you buy them. Frozen ready-mades generally spoil within 24-72 hours dependant upon the time of year and conditions they are stored in.

Shelf-life baits are preserved or stabilised so they can be kept indefinitely without needing freezing, and can easily be left in a rucksack or bait bucket without spoiling. Like any food shelf-life boilies still need to be looked after though, and should be kept, cool, dark and out of direct sunlight. If they get hot and sweat and you see moisture inside the bag they can still spoil.

Debate has raged for 20 years amongst carpers over which is the superior choice, shelf-life or frozen bait, and still the arguments persist. Some carpers have concerns about chemical preservatives in shelf-life bait, fearing carp can smell or taste them, making the bait less attractive. Others have no such concerns and confidently use shelf-life bait, catching plenty of carp and welcoming the convenience of boilies that don't have to be kept frozen and can be left in a rucksack or bucket and used as required. With advancements from the food industry and extensive research and development over many years boilies can be stabilised so they are shelf-life by big bait firms without using harsh chemical preservatives.

A quality shelf-life boilie tastes no different to a frozen ready-made rolled to the same recipe, the only difference is that the shelf-life bait is harder because it is dried for longer to reduce the water content so it won't spoil.

Surprisingly, even the fiercest critics of shelf-life boilies quite happily use commercially available pop-ups - which are shelf-life and sold in pots - and catch plenty of carp on them. If there were big issues over carp smelling and tasting preservatives in shelf-life baits the last place you'd put one was on the hair yet shelf-life pop-ups from all the major manufacturers catch thousands and thousands of carp every year, often on the rods of anglers who insist frozen baits are superior...

Pick shelf-life or frozen boilies depending upon what suits your fishing. Whether they are shelf-life or frozen it's more important to ensure you pick a high quality, attractive bait from an established, reputable manufacturer. This way you'll be sure you've got a bait that has a long standing pedigree for catching carp, whatever format you choose to buy it in.

SIZE MATTERS

BOILIES can be made in any size, from as small as a pea to as big as an orange. Practical angling considerations as well as constraints of commercial and domestic boilie production have led to baits being most widely available in 10-22mm.

The smaller a boilie the longer it takes to manufacture, whether by hand or through machines. Even a small decrease in size, for example from 14 to 12mm significantly increases manufacturing time for the same quantity of bait. Because of this 10mm baits are the smallest widely available boilies and are often more expensive to buy than larger baits because they are more time consuming and costly to produce.

Boilies of 15-20mm are most common size in use on fisheries today, can be catapulted or introduced with throwing sticks to reasonable ranges and also tend to be more selective for carp than smaller boilies. But because of their blanket use, baits of these sizes are also often viewed with suspicion by pressurised carp. Although you pay more for them and they can be more easily eaten by nuisance fish such as bream, roach and tench a simple switch to 10mm boilies can bring lots more fish than relying on more standard 15-20mm baits.

But bigger boilies can also be an advantage. Being heavier, the additional weight of a hook with a 22-24mm boilie is less easy for a carp to detect, and because they are a greater food reward, and more difficult to eat carp can be caught on them very readily. Large boilies are also a big advantage where bream and tench eat more standard size free offerings. The bigger the boilies the less easy it is for any fish other than carp to eat them.

As a rule the smaller a boilie the more bites you will get from all species, making smaller baits ideal when you are visiting venues just once or occasionally and trying to get some action using them in conjunction with other baits like pellets and groundbait.

Bigger boilies work best when fishing the same venue regularly, steadily feeding the same type of bait once or several times a week on your own or as part of a baiting team in a long term baiting campaign to familiarise carp with your chosen boilie recipe as an available, valuable food source.

SHAPING UP

BOILIES don't have to be round, they are only manufactured as balls to make them fly accurately when we bait swims with catapults or throwing sticks.

Although round baits are convenient for us, every bait being uniform in shape makes them incredibly easy for carp to pick up and also spit out again. Changing the shape of your hook bait by using pellet shapes or 'chops' or simply using half baits or double baits on the hair can make a big difference to your results. Baits that aren't round are often eaten in preference to and much more enthusiastically than round balls.

Baiting with different size and shape boilies in the same swim can make it easier to catch carp. Like using different size pellets in your PVA bag filling having different food items of different weights that behave differently makes it much harder for carp to detect the hook bait as being different to the free offerings.

Many boilies are available in different shapes and sizes off the shelf or out of the freezer. Try buying several different types and splitting them down into smaller bags taking a handful of a couple of different sizes and shapes each trip to give you a more effective baited area and several presentation options.

READY ROLLED OR MAKE YOUR OWN?

UNLESS you are a very high volume bait user it is just as easy and much more convenient to buy boilies ready rolled than make your own. There is a cost saving in making your own, mixing eggs, pre-blended base mix and your preferred additives together then rolling and boiling them yourself because you aren't paying for a bait company's employees and machinery to make them for you.

However, to make it a practical proposition you will have to spend money initially on a bait extrusion gun, rolling tables plus all the bottles of additives you require,

and possibly an extra freezer to store the finished bait. The cost of the boilies you produce will drop in real terms but you have to spend money first in order to start saving - such is life!

Added to the smell and mess bait making can cause at home the initial outlay is enough to convince many to pay slightly more for the convenience of picking top quality, effective baits up straight from a tackle shop at their convenience.

BOILIE DIPS

DESIGNED to boost the attraction of boilie hook baits dips are thick liquids that stick to the skin of boilies, leaking off taste and smell around a hook bait after it hits the lake bed.

Most popular boilies have matching dips available infused with the same successful blend of flavours and additives.

Originally designed for low water temperatures dips improve the scent trail from a boilie by hundreds if not thousands of times over to help carp home in on a hook bait and stimulate them to feed. Rather than introducing free offerings and risking over feeding sluggish carp using just one dipped bait in a swim leaves a carp only one bait to choose from - the hook bait.

Baits are left to soak for a few minutes in a dip or simply dunked immediately before casting.
Dips can be used with all manner of hook baits not just boilies and have applications all year, with groundbaits, stick mixes and PVA bags.

One of the biggest drawbacks of using dips to help catch carp is the mess it creates. Fishing baits out of jars or bottles of dip is a recipe for everything from sticky hands to sticky sleeping bags, and dip bottles are also notorious for leaking - which can ruin clothes, tackle or even expensive cameras and radios inside rucksacks and carryalls.

Fox Glug Pots feature a rubber seal on the inside of the screw lid to create an effective watertight barrier and prevent dips leaking in transit. The inner bait cage clips on to the side of the jar, allowing the dip to drain away and baits to be more easily removed and mounted on a rig - which saves chasing baits round the pot with needles, spoons or fingers!

PASTE

Carp eat soft food items much more enthusiastically than hard ones, and softer boilies tend to be more successful than rock hard baits.

A great tactic to improve the pull of your boilie hook baits is to mould a small covering of boilie paste around the outside of the bait before casting out. If you make your own bait keep a lump of unboiled paste to one side and freeze it in small egg sized lumps to take each trip. Alternatively, many major manufacturers such as Mainline and Essential Baits sell frozen paste to match their ranges of frozen ready-made boilies. Again, break the paste into smaller, session sized lumps and take one out the freezer with your boilies each session.

Releasing attractors into the water more effectively than a boilie with a tough skin, a paste covering around hook baits is another way to mimic a bait that has been immersed for a long period, softened and begun to break down - which is often treated as a safe meal by a pressurised carp.

WASHED OUT BAITS

THE longer a boilie is left on the bottom without being eaten the more water it absorbs, the softer it becomes and the less strongly it smells, as its flavours and attractors slowly dissipate into the water around it.

With most carpers reeling in and changing their hook baits for fresh boilies out the bag every few hours or after a night without action it's thought that on heavily fished venues carp very quickly learn that the soft, less strongly smelling boilies that have been in water for long periods are safest to eat.

We can leave hook baits in position for long periods and let them gradually soften and the flavour to wash out until they are viewed with less caution by the carp, but it's easier and quicker to let baits soak in lake water before or whilst you are fishing, to allow you to fish with hook baits that have the appearance of being old washed out baits.

At the start of a session fill a bucket with a few inches of lake water. Don't ever use tap water. Stick a handful of boilies in, and leave the baits in the sun to warm the water and speed up the 'ageing' process. Even if regularly feeding more free offerings, using a washed out hook bait on the hair is a great tactic. Single, washed out hook baits can be incredibly successful, especially for bigger carp.

Because washed out baits soften when they are immersed for long periods before being used, big 16-20mm boilies are a better choice, preventing them being pecked or pulled off the hair by nuisance fish.

FRESH IS BEST

BOILIES taken from the freezer are best kept frozen or cool through the duration of your stay. Almost all boilies are bound and skinned with fresh eggs, and you wouldn't need to leave a cooked egg out in the sun for long before you wouldn't fancy eating it. Treat frozen boilies as you would fresh food to eat yourself.

Because there are no hard and fast rules in carp angling, perversely there are a handful of frozen ready-made boilies that seem to produce better results when they have slightly spoiled and either gone sticky or white with mould. These are very isolated cases where as they spoil the ingredients emit stronger food signals and become more attractive to a carp. In the long term you will always catch more by making an effort to keep your boilies in the best condition.

Fox produce a huge range of bags with heat reflective linings storing anything from a couple of kilos of boilies for a day session or overnight trip to ten kilos or more for a longer stay Adding freezer blocks and keeping cooler bags in a bivvy and out of direct sunshine will keep bait in great condition for several days.

AIR DRYING

IN the same way that foods we eat can be preserved by drying, frozen boilies can be dried to extend their life. Reducing moisture level in any food prevents bacterial action and stops it spoiling.

Drying baits is a tactic used by fans of frozen ready-made boilies who need to store baits through long sessions where freezer facilities aren't available and it's impractical for cool bags and freezer blocks to keep bait fresh. Air drying is a great advantage when travelling abroad for week long holidays or sessions of three days or more.

To dry boilies effectively they need to be spread in a warm, well ventilated place like a shed or garage to allow moisture to slowly evaporate. Baits should be secure from pests like mice, pets and children. The smell of drying boilies in a house is unpleasant and best avoided.

Dry baits during periods of settled warmer weather in the summer rather than through the winter when there's more moisture in the air and baits can become damp.

Spreading baits thinly on towels or sheets will allow them to dry, but it's best to allow air to circulate all around them by spreading them on trays. You can use old bread trays or buy purpose designed boilie drying trays. Turn the baits or move them around on the trays every few days.

Depending upon the temperature baits will be fully dried in ten days to two weeks. They will have shrunk by several millimetres, become very hard, lighter in colour and weight.

Even when thoroughly dried boilies can still spoil if they are stored badly. If kept in sealed bags or buckets in strong sunlight or changing temperatures dried baits will still sweat and ultimately spoil.

Fox Deluxe Air Dry Bags feature strong webbing carry straps and tough zips. Large diameter mesh allows air to circulate, keeping baits in optimum condition.

In good weather air dry bags can either be hung in trees or on storm poles to allow baits to air. Store them back in a bivvy overnight to prevent baits getting damp overnight, and attracting rats.

Air dried baits can be used in throwing sticks without splitting, but because they are lighter in weight range is reduced compared to fresh baits of the same size.

Bait drills will be required to mount air dried boilies on the hair. Trying to push standard needles through rock hard dried baits is a recipe for snapped needles or slipping and pushing a needle into your hand.

Although air dried baits are tough they also absorb water rapidly, softening quickly in a swim and becoming much more attractive.

CHAPTER 15

PARTICLE BAITS

PARTICLE BAITS

CARP probably have the broadest taste of any freshwater fish and will eat all manner of seeds, beans, nuts and pulses - commonly referred to as particle baits or mass baits.

Pioneered in the 70s by famous carper Rod Hutchinson, particle fishing changed the way we look at baits and application of baits for carp. Instead of single balls of paste or a handful of free offerings, Rod advocated heavy use of small baits that encouraged intensive, competitive feeding amongst numbers of fish.

Many of the particle baits he pioneered remain all time greats and will continue to catch carp for as long as they are used, but it was their application that was often as critical to their success as the type of bait itself. For the first time anglers began to realise just how much bait carp could and would eat if given the opportunity.

The popularity of particle baits has dropped with the development of the boilie market and the huge boom in using commercial feed pellets but particles still have plenty to offer. Primarily they offer a cheap bait option for those on a budget. For the same price as one kilo of quality frozen ready-made boilies you can buy 15 kg of hempseed, that when soaked and boiled will produce more like 25 kg of bait - enough to last many sessions and catch numbers of carp.

There is a world of particle baits to explore and carp have been caught on everything from broad beans to bulgar wheat and lupin seeds. But over the years a handful of particle baits have proven to be real winners.

PRE-COOKED OR PREPARE YOUR OWN?

WE live in an age of convenience, and no longer do you have to soak and boil particle baits yourself. Several major manufacturers supply popular baits like hemp, pigeon mix and tiger nuts pre-cooked on the tackle shop shelf.

Although they cost more than preparing your own, these baits are sealed and cooked inside the tins and jars, ensuring all the oils, sugars and natural attractants are retained making them superior baits. Hempseed cooked in tins and jars is much oilier than hemp prepared at home through traditional soaking and boiling. Despite the cost many anglers prefer convenience particle baits for this reason.

Pre-cooked particles have a substantial shelf-life as long as jars and tins are kept unopened, and can be carried in rucksacks or left in the car to be used when required, making them ideal for long sessions or trips abroad.

With the benefits of additives like chilli having been widely documented in recent seasons, it hasn't taken long for bait companies to also supply pre-prepared particles with proven additives like chilli powder and flakes, garlic and intense sweeteners, giving even greater taste and smell to stimulate carp to feed.

TIGER NUTS

THE most famous and effective particle bait of all time for carp, tiger nuts aren't nuts at all but are small, very sweet tubers eaten by both humans as a delicacy and animals as a feed product. They are famed for their ability to catch the hardest carp time after time and would figure close to the top of many experienced carpers' list of favourite baits.

What makes tiger nuts so successful is hotly debated. Small, dark, wrinkled and varying in size from a garden pea to the diameter of a small boilie they are soaked for 24 hours then boiled for 30 minutes, the nuts absorbing water until they have a smoother appearance. Their hard, crunchy texture is supposed by many to be a key part of their appeal. More likely is that the natural sugars found within tiger nuts are extremely attractive. Despite their sweet taste, to us tigers smell very little.

But there's no question carp smell them and respond to them from much longer distances than other baits.

Concealing tiger nuts in tanks or ponds will have carp tearing the bottom up to find them on smell alone, without ever having eaten one.

For all their appeal tiger nuts have little nutritional value to carp. A carp's inability to fully digest tiger nuts is another contributory factor to their success. Whole or part nuts are excreted all over the lake after carp have eaten them, and in turn are eaten again by other carp. Carp also become used to finding part or whole tigers in safe havens such as snags where fish spend long periods resting and digesting.

Tiger nuts produce best when fished in small quantities. A stringer or small PVA bag with a dozen tiger nuts is tremendously effective,

particularly over a handful of a smaller particle bait like hemp or even small pellets. They produce carp even through the coldest weather and so attractive are they, experienced carpers will confidently use single tiger nut hook baits with no free offerings.

TIGER NUT PREPARATION

LIKE all particle baits tiger nuts must be prepared correctly. They require soaking for 24 hours to absorb water, then boiling for 30 minutes. Tiger nuts will never soften but a baiting needle should pass easily through them. They can be left to cool and kept in their own water for up to a week. In warm weather they begin to develop a 'snotty' feel and the water becomes thick and sticky as the natural sugars they contain begin to ferment. Some carpers feel they are at their most effective when left to mature for several days before use.

SWEETCORN AND MAIZE

ONE of the most important cereal food crops in the world maize and its close genetic relative sweetcorn both make fantastic carp baits.

Sweetcorn is highly visible, incredibly attractive thanks to high levels of the amino acid Lysine and instantly accepted. Softer and sweeter than maize, corn is the more popular bait, and is often included in spod mixes, method mixes and groundbaits. Such is its appeal carp can often be seen actively picking out the grains of corn out from areas baited with several different feeds. Tinned sweetcorn in salted and sweetened water is widely accepted as a superior bait to frozen corn, but carp happily mop up corn whatever the brand.

Maize is similar to sweetcorn, but a tougher kernel that requires soaking and boiling before use. Being such a huge international food crop maize is dirt cheap, costing at most £10 per 25 kg sack when bought from bait dealers rather than feed suppliers.

A staple carp bait particularly on the Continent and in the United States and Canada where it can be used in large quantities to feed and hold large numbers of big carp, it is also a favourite in the UK, although more commonly these days is used as a hook bait rather than a feed.

Being much tougher than its sister bait sweetcorn even a single grain of maize can be hair rigged and safely cast out indefinitely, knowing that nuisance fish won't strip the bait from the rig - the one drawback of softer corn. In a swim containing sweetcorn free offerings a grain of maize on the hair is readily accepted as the same food.

MAIZE PREPARATION

UNLIKE corn which needs no preparation and is fished straight out of the tin, maize needs soaking and boiling before use.

Add a kilo of maize to a pan of water, adding six table spoons of sugar and one of salt. Leave the maize to soak for 24 hours, then bring the water to the boil and simmer for 20-30 minutes until the grains have softened. A baiting needle will easily pass through them and they will have a rich, sweet and slightly salty taste.

Maize keeps for several days without refrigeration, left in the same water it was cooked in. Only when the water has a soured smell are the grains past their best.

TOP TIP
CREAM OF THE CROP

LIQUIDISED or creamed corn is available in tins in good supermarkets. Added to spod mixes it forms an attractive milky cloud in the water as the bait sinks, helping pull fish from long distances.

HEMP

FIRST used as a bait in the UK on the River Thames at the turn of the 20th century by immigrant workers from Europe hempseed is loved by almost every freshwater fish, from roach to barbel, to tench, bream and most of all, carp.

There is much debate over the attraction of hempseed. The seed of the marijuana plant, in the early days of its use there were fears hempseed drugged fish. It is also suggested hemp mimics the small snails found in abundance on many rich gravel pits. Carp tear the bottom up for hemp because it is one of nature's most complete food sources with an outstanding nutritional profile rich in essential fatty acids and a balanced breakdown of major food groups.

Hemp provokes an amazingly intense feeding reaction, fish returning to a baited area time and time again to search out every last grain. Being cheap, easy to prepare and outstanding at holding carp in a swim for long periods hemp has become a core ingredient for many spod mixes.

IT'S A BIND

CRUSHED hemp can be added to spod mixes, method mixes and stick mixes to improve their pull. Rich in attractive hemp oil, crushed hemp releases a milky cloud in water and boasts significant binding properties, reducing spod spill and improving the texture of method balls.

HEMP PREPARATION

HEMP needs to be soaked for 12-14 hours, then brought to the boil. As it reaches the boil remove it from the heat and allow the hemp to cool in the same water. The seeds will split to reveal the white kernel inside. Once cooked, hemp keeps in its own water for several days, convenient during longer sessions.

PIGEON MIX

DEVELOPED for rearing racing pigeons, pigeon mixes are blends of many different types and sizes of seeds, peas and beans. Similar concoctions are sometimes sold by bait companies as mixed particle or parti-blend. The most effective pigeon mixes such as Red Band have aniseed extract infused into the seeds - carp love the smell and taste of aniseed.

With different shapes, sizes, tastes and densities of feed items pigeon mixes get carp grubbing around for long periods, making it another favourite for spod mixes and heavy baiting situations.

Another cheap bait, 25 kg of dry pigeon mix can also be bought for not much more than the price of a kilo of quality boilies.

PREPARING PIGEON MIX

ONE of the easiest particles of all to prepare pigeon mix or parti-blend requires no prior soaking, just scalding with boiling water. One third fill a bucket with parti-blend and cover to twice the depth with boiling water, allowing the seeds room to swell. As soon as the water is cool the pigeon mix is ready to use.

HOW MUCH?

THE smaller the bait the more can be introduced. Seeds like hemp and pigeon mix can be baited very heavily where harder baits like nuts work better when lightly baited.

The particle boom of the 70s showed that carp could consume vast quantities of feed. The great Rod Hutchinson would use buckets and buckets of particles and catch as many carp in days as others recorded in a season. Much of the success was due to such heavy bait application, a tactic that hadn't been exploited.

Today, with heavier baiting than ever it is wise to feed less aggressively, but at certain times of the year, in good weather or when time is on your side particle baits, particularly small ones can score well when fed very heavily.

GETTING THEM OUT

PARTICLES are less easy to feed than boilies or pellets. At short ranges they can be tightly grouped using a catapult with a large pouch. Baiting spoons are useful for spreading small baits at short range. Beyond very close range particles need to be spodded to feed accurately.

The liquid that surrounds soaked particles contains oils, sugars and other attractants. Using the full or half blanking inserts in Fox TB spods ensures the liquid doesn't drip out before casting, adding weight for improved distance and adding pull to the baited area by dropping attractive liquid with the particles as they leave the spod.

SALT

ALMOST all particles are improved by salt, added directly to the water that they are soaked and boiled in or mixed it with pre-prepared baits.

Salt in a carp's diet is necessary for regulation of water balance in the body. Salt is also a taste sensation carp recognise and respond to, and improves dissipation of attractors in water.

There is no minimum or maximum inclusion level, but carp's taste receptors are so powerful they will know the salt is there even if you don't. Try adding 1-2 teaspoons per dry kilo of particle. Sea salt is preferable to rock salt as it doesn't contain any chemical anti-caking agents.

CHILLI

CARP respond enthusiastically to the hot taste of chilli and other spices. Either add a sprinkle of chilli flakes or add 1-2 teaspoons of chilli powder to each dry kilo of particle when it is soaked to give a hot twang to your bait bucket.

SWEETENERS

IF not using salt, particle baits can also be improved by the addition of a sweetener. You can use any type of sweetener, from granulated sugar to syrup but 1ml per dry kilo of any Talin based sweetener is hard to beat, especially in tiger nuts.

CHAPTER 16

DYNAMITE BAITS

MARINE HALIBUT PELLETS

Attracts Big Carp
more agressively
than high oil
pellets
without competing

TOTALLY CARP FRIENDLY

PELLETS

PELLETS of all shapes, sizes and types have become one of the most effective and widely used carp baits of recent times.

Although not a new carp bait - trout pellet paste was catching carp back in the 70s - their use has become so widespread in the last decade that they justifiably challenge boilies as the most popular carp bait of all.

What makes pellets such a great carp bait? Packed with protein rich fishmeals for growth and tissue repair, oils for energy, vitamins and minerals for health and appetite stimulators to encourage feeding they are a near perfect diet and incredibly attractive to fish of all species.

Some of the most successful pellets are those developed for commercially rearing fish species such as halibut or trout. So nutritious are many commercial feed pellets that they boast a 1:1 food conversion ratio, meaning for every kilo of pellets fed the fish convert that kilo of pellet to a kilo of flesh through growth - a remarkable statistic.

WHICH PELLET?

THERE are huge differences between the pellets available off the shelf. Some are fantastically effective fish catchers, others average at best. A high price tag and big company name isn't a guarantee of getting the best bait.

MARINE PELLETS

MARINE pellets is a generic term used by bait and feed companies to describe halibut pellets. Halibut are a giant saltwater flatfish species, and are very tricky to commercially farm for the table. Halibut pellets have been developed to encourage these fussy flatfish to feed in a farm environment, and are packed with appetite stimulators and palatants. They have a huge protein content at around 50 per cent and typically an oil content of 25 per cent. Almost single handedly halibut pellets have changed specimen fishing, and they have become the bait of choice for not just big carp, but also barbel, chub, tench and bream. Virtually every coarse fish species eats halibut pellets with enthusiasm such good food are they. If you were limited to using one variety of pellet, halibut pellets would be first choice.

They sell for around £4 per kilo, but in bulk can be bought for as little as £30-35 for 25 kilos, and are commonly available in 3, 4, 6, 8, 10, 14 and 21mm size's.

TROUT PELLETS

Trout pellets were used in the earliest pastes and boilies after being ground down and mixed with eggs. They remain a great carp bait, although the popularity of halibuts has seen them used less widely. Lighter in appearance than halibut pellets they typically contain 40 per cent protein and around 20 per cent oil. Trout pellets are cheaper but carp still love them. They have the added advantage of being available as a floating feed as well - ideal for surface fishing (see chapter 10). Trout pellet feeds, floating or sinking, are commonly available in 3-11mm size's.

CARP PELLETS

Major feed manufacturers also produce carp pellets, designed to fulfil all of a growing carp's nutritional needs. In short, they are the equivalent of the perfect pill, carp will thrive on them without any additional feeds.

Although carp eat pellets designed for their nutritional needs, the irony is that given a choice they much prefer to eat more oil rich trout and halibut pellets. In tank situations you can feed carp a mix of carp pellets and halibut pellets and they will hoover them all up, then spit out the carp pellets and eat the halibut pellets. Carp pellets are the only pellets allowed on some venues but where you have the option, you'll catch more using trout and halibut pellets.

BREAKDOWN PELLETS

Pellets are also used as feeds for other farmed animals, not just trout or halibut. There are plenty of cheap compressed pellets designed for sheep, cows and even chickens. Typically lighter in colour and weight, low diameter with a slender stick like appearance they break down in minutes. Although attractive to carp, releasing attractors into the water rapidly even in very low temperatures they have nowhere near the same pull or nutritional profile of a halibut or trout pellet. Many breakdown pellets have flavours and colours added to improve their appeal to both anglers and fish.

CUSTOM PELLETS

MOST mainstream bait manufacturers supply pellets, often to match their most successful boilie mixes or including their most popular additives. They vary from off the shelf feed pellets simply soaked in flavours and attractors to cheap breakdown pellets with custom additives to top quality tailor made pellets using proven ingredients and additives unique to the bait company.

Stick with established, reputable bait companies like Mainline and Nutrabaits to ensure you get the best quality. Mainline's Response Pellet are a range of dedicated pellets using the liquid foods found in their food baits such as Grange CSL, Activ-8, Fusion and Pulse.

Hemp pellets are another common custom pellet, although quality can vary enormously. Some cheaper hemp pellets contain a substantial quantity of fibrous waste material from processing hemp plants, with little or no hempseed.

Mainline Hemp Pellets are top quality, being pure crushed hempseed compressed into a pellet, dissolving quickly in all temperatures.

HAIR RIGGING HALIBUTS

DRILLING out large pellets for the hair can be tricky, pellets often splitting as the drill emerges.

Fresh pellets drill more easily - don't buy old, dusty bags of pellets. Pellets are shelf-life but can deteriorate. To store them in best condition keep them cool and dark in airtight bags or buckets.

Keep the drill straight and drill slowly, withdrawing the drill occasionally to stop it clogging with pellet dust.

Because pellets are harder than boilies a standard hair stop can't pull into the skin of a pellet. With a larger diameter hole from being drilled it only takes minimal movement of the pellet on the hair for a standard stop to come loose allowing the bait to be pulled off.

Fox Pellet Pegs are purpose designed stops that pull tightly into the hole made by a drill, reducing water uptake and preventing the pellet being pulled off the rig. They are available in 11, 13 and 21mm to suit different size hook baits.

HOW TO HAIR RIG A PELLET

1. Fresh pellets drill most easily. Pellets of 14 or 21mm make ideal hook baits.

2. Use a fine diameter Fox Pellet Drill and drill slowly, lengthways through the pellet.

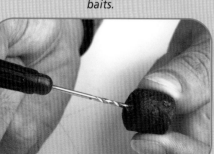

3. Once the drill is through use a larger 1.5mm drill to enlarge the hole to accept the stop.

4. Fox Pellet Pegs prevent them being pulled off the hair.

HIGH OIL DANGERS?

DEBATE still rolls on as to whether the oil content of pellets can be a long term danger to carp health.

There is no firm scientific evidence that has been presented to show that high oil feeds like trout and halibut pellets are a danger to carp health. Some fisheries ban pellets other than low oil carp pellets because they have concerns about the health of their stocks, and often only allow you to use the specific pellets they sell on site. It is a legitimate management tool to monitor feeds being introduced to a fishery but the cynics might observe that it also has the knock on effect of increasing profit from bait sales at a venue.

Anecdotally, extremely heavy use of high oil pellets over short periods does seem to have a longer term effect on fisheries, producing huge catches then much reduced sport for several weeks to follow. But these are instances where the quantities being used are measured in sacks not kilos - a very rare situation and not at representative of the situation on most fisheries where carp have a varied diet including natural food plus a selection of baits to supplement that natural larder.

On almost every fishery that is sufficiently balanced to grow and sustain big carp regular use of high oil pellets has no detrimental effect. They are a valuable food source and help carp grow and remain in tip top condition.

TOP TIP

IF farmed fish aren't successfully weaned on to an artificial diet at the beginning of their life they die, so feeds to rear juvenile fish have to be the most attractive of all. Fry crumb feeds are like a coarse dust, but each grain is a nutritionally complete package. They make outstanding baits, bringing an incredibly strong feeding response, and make excellent PVA bag or stick fillings and groundbait additives.

BALLING UP PELLETS

PELLETS can be quickly introduced into a swim in large quantities by softening them with water and balling them up like groundbait. Firing balls of pellet out with a groundbait catapult like the Fox Swinghead is much quicker than spodding. Softened pellet is a great feed when PVA bagging, alternatively mould the dampened pellet firmly around a Method feeder.

1. Put a couple of kilos of small 3-6mm pellets in a groundbait bowl or bucket. The Evolution Method Bowl flattens down when not in use for easy storage.

2. Add a mugful of boiling water, and mix it thoroughly around the bowl with a wooden spoon or baiting scoop.

3. Leave the pellets to stand for 15 minutes, giving them an occasional shake. They should be lighter coloured, soft and with a gentle squeeze form a ball.

4. Don't make the balls too big. Balls the size of a tangerine will catapult substantial distances. Make them up in advance so you get into a rhythm when catapulting, and keep the balls the same size so they fly the same.

OVERNIGHT PELLET RIG

One of a pellet's key features - that it softens and dissolves quickly in water to release valuable food signals - prevents them from being used more widely as hook baits. Boilie hook baits over baited areas of pellets are often not as productive as using pellets on the hair but few anglers want to sit behind rods worrying if their pellet hook bait has dissolved or been whittled away by smaller fish.

1. Carefully drill a pellet out then slip a piece of large diameter shrink tube (commonly sold as Bait Armour) over it.

2. Hold a lighter just below the tube until it begins to shrink down, turning the pellet as the tube contracts to ensure the pellet is tightly gripped all the way around.

3. Thread on a hair and insert a Fox Pellet Peg. Because the pellet is shrink wrapped it can't readily absorb water. Your hook bait smells and tastes identical to free pellets but can be left in water for 24-48 hours without fear of it being pulled off.

CHAPTER 17
PVA

PVA

PVA products have arguably had the biggest impact on carp catching tactics of any bait or rig development since the hair rig and boilies.

Poly Vinyl Alcohol is a water soluble substance widely used in agriculture and healthcare that can be manufactured into string, tape, bags and mesh. In carp angling PVA's ability to dissolve to nothing within seconds of being exposed to water gives it incredible potential to help us group free offerings directly around a hook bait.

Unless fishing directly under your feet and dropping loose feed over a rig, you will never achieve the same accuracy by catapulting or even spodding free offerings as when using PVA. It allows us to position the tiniest of pellets, chopped baits, maggots or groundbaits around a hook bait even if we are fishing at ranges in excess of 100 yards, enhancing the attraction around a rig by hundreds if not thousands of times.

Such precise grouping of feeds is devastating compared with casting out single baits on a rig - so much so that looking around popular carp venues it is becoming rare to see many carpers cast out without some sort of PVA involved around the rig.

PVA bags are the most commonly used form of PVA, and come in a variety of different forms for different situations, bait types and presentations. Twinned with PVA string, mesh and tape they offer us a world of possibilities for catching carp quicker and more easily than when fishing with rigs carrying hook baits alone.

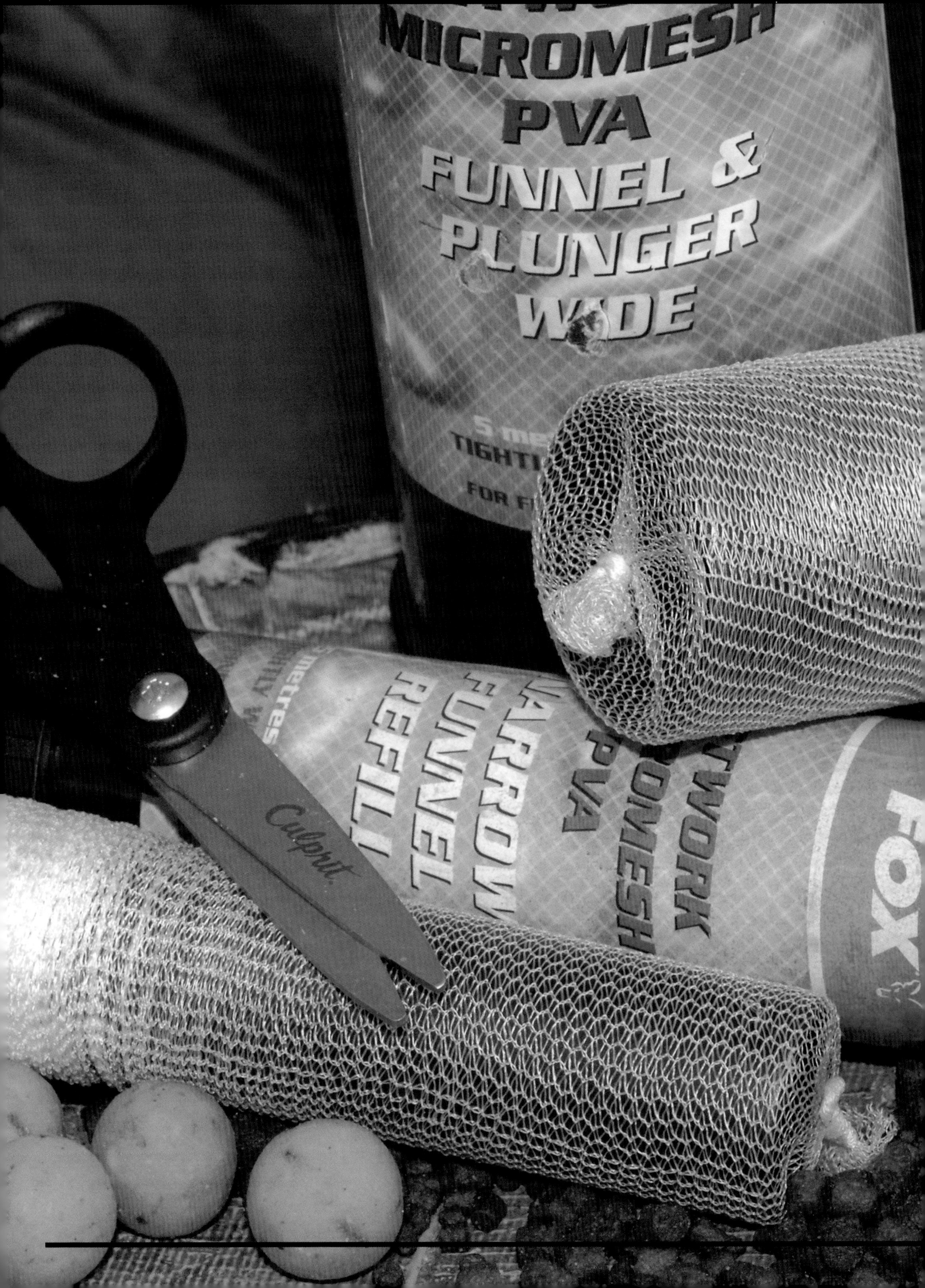
MICROMESH
PVA
FUNNEL &
PLUNGER
WIDE
PVA
Culprit
FOX

COBWEB PVA BAGS

THE most popular PVA bag system of all, cobweb bags are made from continuous tubes of PVA stocking mesh stored on hollow plastic tubes. It's the quickest and easiest system of making PVA parcels of bait, different diameters of tube allowing us to make different size bags.

Cobweb bags are the best choice for well stocked venues where there is likely to be regular action. They can be tied in advance while waiting for takes or even the day or night before a session as long as they are kept dry in a sealed bag or container. Each time you catch a fish or recast it's as simple as nicking a fresh bag over the hook and you're fishing again in seconds. In contrast tying solid sheet style PVA bags is more time consuming and can lead to much more time without baits in the water, which on busy waters means less bites and fewer carp.

Because they can be made very small and tightly compacted, cobweb bags can also be cast long distances using the right end tackles, allowing us to introduce feed around the hook bait at distances impossible to cast with larger solid sheet style PVA bags.

Cobweb bags can also be quickly varied in size and filling. Even using the same diameter loading tube cobweb bags can be tied as small as a ten pence piece or as big as a golf ball, allowing us to vary our presentation and react to changing conditions.

TOP TIP

Fox Network PVA comes in two varieties. Use the larger Anti-Ladder mesh for boilies, broken boilies, larger dried particle baits and pellets. Micromesh Anti-Ladder has a much smaller weave, allowing maggots, groundbaits and micro-pellets to be used in bags without them escaping or falling through during loading.

TYING COBWEB BAGS

1. Check the PVA mesh is knotted at the base of the tube then put a pinch of your feed - here we're using pellets - into the palm of your hand and pour it down the tube.

2. Holding the PVA mesh tight to the end of the loading tube push the plunger down the tube to compress the bait.

3. Stop gripping the PVA on the tube and gently push the parcel of bait out of the end of the tube. You should have created a small pellet parcel the size of a golf ball.

4. Slide the PVA mesh and bag down off the tube, and twist the loose PVA directly above the top of the bag.

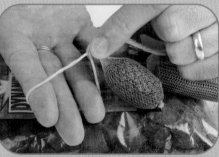

5. Wrap the twisted mesh around three fingers and poke the bag through the hole you create between them.

6. Use your two fingers to trap the twisted PVA on top of the bag, pulling the loose end slowly to tie the bag off. Tight bags cast more easily and dissolve quicker.

7. Snip the bag off, then tie an overhand knot in the bottom of the mesh in readiness for the next bag to be filled.

8. Cobweb bags are nicked over the hook before casting. Hook the centre of the bag. Pushing the hook point through the knots can impede hooking.

SOLID SHEET PVA BAGS

THE bags that started the PVA revolution in the early 90s, solid sheet style PVA bags have a key difference to cobweb bags - they allow the complete end tackle including lead and hook length to be put inside the bag and surrounded by feed.

With a hook bait, hook, hair, hook length and lead inside a bag we create an almost perfect go anywhere, catch a carp presentation. The tight grouping of a significant amount of feed focuses a carp's feeding right on top of the hook bait, and brings about quite an aggressive response - the free bait and hook bait often disappearing down a carp's mouth in a couple of mouthfuls.

There is no possibility of a tangle, and no matter how long the hair or complex the rig you want to use it will offer perfect presentation as soon as the PVA dissolves to reveal the rig and bait. Because the contents of the bag is protected on the cast we can also confidently use a greater variety of hook baits than when casting, knowing they will reach the lake bed in perfect condition - even worms!

Solid PVA bags can be cast just about anywhere and still offer an effective presentation which is their number one appeal. Sinking more slowly than standard lead end tackles because of the bag's shape a solid PVA bag settles lightly over silt or over silkweed. Because a finished solid bag is rounded they also tend to settle nicely between stalks of emerging weed or lilies.
You can be sure that your hook length won't be hung up on leaves or stems and you'll be fishing effectively even in areas that can't be fished with more orthodox end tackles and hook baits.

There are disadvantages to solid PVA bags. They are much more sizeable than cobweb bags in order to allow rigs to be tucked inside them, reducing casting distances and demanding more powerful rods and heavier lines to cast them safely. They are also more readily affected by cross winds. Range is also more limited, only with a heavy leader, strong rods, good technique and a well tied bag is it possible to consistently fish at range of beyond 70-80 yards with most solid style PVA bags.

They also take longer to tie - although you get much quicker with practice - and require care to be taken that no moisture remains around your lead or rig, otherwise bags can easily blister and dissolve from contact with damp rig bits before you even cast them out. However, a well tied solid PVA bag is aerodynamic, casts true, and with care completely conceals and camouflages your rig in a pile of highly attractive food particles that can be cast almost anywhere on any type of venue and offer you a great chance of action.

1. Fade Away bags use carefully selected film to offer fast breakdown in the coldest water temperatures yet won't dissolve as the bag sinks through deeper water at summer temperatures.

5. Lower the hook bait and hook down the funnel into the bag, ensuring the hook length runs through the slot. Tuck the hook bait into one corner of the bag and lay the hook length along the top of the pellets.

TYING SOLID PVA BAGS

2. The ideal end tackle for solid PVA bags is a 2-3 oz in-line lead with a short 8-12cm braided Reflex hook length and small Arma Point hook. Make sure the whole end tackle is towelled dry and any water inside the lead blown out and dried off.

3. Slide a Fade Away bag on to the Ezee Loader and tuck the lead into the retaining cup at the top of the funnel. Leave the hook length hanging on the outside of the funnel initially.

4. Solid bags are easiest to make with very small pellets as a filling. They leave fewer air pockets and create a denser bag. Sprinkle micro pellets down the funnel until you have a layer around 5mm deep along the base of the bag.

6. Add another sprinkle of pellets to cover the hook and hook length then position the lead in the centre of the bag. It should only be sitting 1.5-2cm away from the nose of the bag.

7. Add more pellets, pushing down with a finger tip to ensure they are compacted around the lead and there are no large air pockets. Leave at least 3-4cm of PVA empty at the neck of the bag.

8. Remove the filled bag from the Ezee Loader by sliding it down off the funnel, ensuring the main line behind the lead follows and is gently pulled through the slot in the side of the funnel.

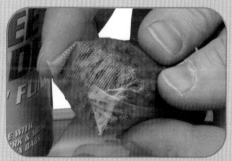

9. Holding the neck of the bag, push it down into the palm of your hand several times to compact the pellets still further. Gather and twist the PVA at the neck to close the bag as tightly as possible.

10. Holding the twisted neck of the bag tie a loop of PVA tape or string around the very base of the twisted PVA at the top of the bag filling. Secure with a granny knot, then repeat with a second loop and knot. Trim the loose ends.

11. Gently pull one of the bottom corners of the bag. Pluck gently at the PVA until you have created a triangular flap of empty PVA. Using a wet finger or damp cotton bud moisten it.

12. Pull the triangular flap down and across the base of the bag and using firm finger pressure stick it to the side. If it doesn't stick after a second or two you need to moisten it more.

13. Repeat with the other corner and you will create a much more aerodynamic rounded bottom bag that will cast more easily. Your bag is now ready to go.

14. Loaded solid PVA bags are much heavier than cobweb bags. With a 2.25 oz in-line lead a Fade Away Bullet bag will weigh 4 oz. For safety we recommend a minimum of 15 lb main line to prevent crack-offs when using solid bags.

LIQUID TRICKS WITH PVA

ALTHOUGH readily dissolving in water, PVA will not dissolve when in contact with other liquids with zero or minimal water content. We can use this to our advantage as there are plenty of liquids that carp find attractive that are not water based. Good examples are fish oils and a huge percentage of the dips and bait boosters available from bait companies.

Cobweb bags can simply be dunked into jars or bottles of PVA friendly dip before casting to enhance the attraction around the hook bait without introducing any more excessive free offerings.

After adding the base layer of pellets, hook length and lead use a syringe (without needle) to squirt 10-20ml of PVA friendly dip into solid style PVA bags before filling to the top with pellets and tying off.

IMPREGNATED PVA

AN innovation from Fox, impregnated PVA uses attractive food liquids within the PVA film. As the PVA dissolves it releases proven attractors around the hook bait. This also helps mask any chemical signal that is unique to PVA, and may be a source of danger to carp repeatedly caught using bags.

Mainline-Fox PVA uses the very best liquid food additives from proven Mainline boilies such as Activ-8, Activ Maple-8, Fusion and Pro-Active Pineapple. The liquid foods that are key to the success of these baits can only boost the attraction of your bag and its contents.

Available as narrow and wide Network mesh or narrow, standard and bullet Fade Away solid bags, Mainline-Fox impregnated bags offer the versatility for any modern PVA presentation, with added pulling power.

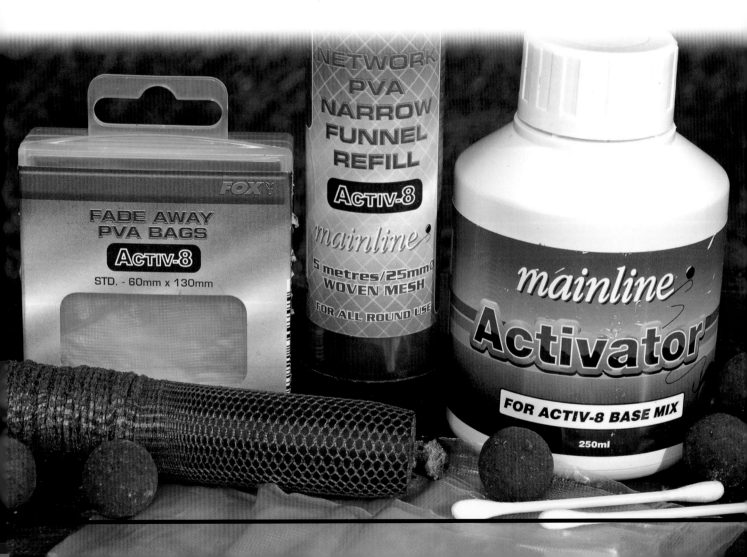

OILY PELLET BAGS

Carp love fish oils. They are highly attractive, a fantastic protein sparing energy source and rich in nutritional Omega 3 fatty acids. Fish oils are a key ingredient in many pellets, and boosting the level of fish oil in your pellets through the summer brings an even more enthusiastic feeding response and noticeably more takes.

Add oil to your pellet bucket and mix until the pellets are all evenly coated and glistening. Salmon oil, cod liver oil, Tackle Box Ming Oil and Mainline Fosoil are all recommended. You can also include a sprinkle of marine pellet groundbait or Mainline Pro-Active crushed hemp or tiger nut stick mix.

Then tie cobweb or solid sheet style bags as normal using your oily pellet mix. Although not a problem in summer temperatures the oil will reduce the dissolve time of the PVA slightly, making it a less effective tactic through autumn and winter.

When a carp noses your oily pellet PVA bag filling, droplets of oil disturbed will rise to the surface above the hook bait and create a flat spot on the water, telling you action shouldn't be long in coming.

It's a huge confidence booster knowing that fish are eating the contents of your bags, and there is carp activity in the swim.

If you repeatedly see flat spots appearing over your bags and aren't getting takes it also tells you that a small rig change like a shorter hook length or change of hook bait is required to hook the carp feeding on the contents of the bag.

Using liquids to improve the pull of PVA bags can be a messy business. Use Fox Glug Pots to safely store fish oils and PVA friendly dips. The screw top with integral rubber seal prevents leaks and spillages.

FEATURES:
- Leak proof screw down cap
- Plastic basket for easy ac to bait
- Basket holder for non bait removal
- Holds approx. 60 x

PVA BAGGING WITH HELICOPTER RIGS

A MAJOR drawback of helicopter rigs is that without thought they don't lend themselves to PVA bag presentations. Because the hook length is trapped by a rubber bead over silicone tube on the lead core, adding any weight to the end of the hook length by nicking a PVA bag of pellets or chopped boilies on to it simply bounces the bead off the silicone on the cast or on impact with water. If the stop bead moves it allows the hook length to run free up the leader and main line. Your hook length and bag won't land next to the lead and the hooking efficiency of your end tackle will be reduced to nil.

Switching the style of lead you use is an easy way to allow you to attach cobweb PVA bags to a helicopter end tackle without affecting its hooking efficiency.

1. Take a 2-2.5 oz in-line lead and snip off the rubber insert where it exits the rear of the lead.

2. Thread it on to a ready spliced lead core leader as if constructing a standard in-line end tackle, followed by a ring swivel threaded through the ring rather than the eye and a camo flexi bead.

3. Slide a 15mm length of 0.5mm silicone down the leader to 1-2cm above the lead and push the rubber flexi bead over the top of it to semi-fix it in position. The hook length is tied to the ring swivel on the lead core leader as usual.

4. Tie a cobweb PVA bag from Network Micromesh and leave a 6-8cm tag end of PVA mesh above the knotted top of the bag.

5. Pass the tag end of PVA mesh through the swivel protruding from the insert of the in-line lead and pull the bag to sit up tight below the lead.

6. Tie the bag to the swivel using a couple of granny knots and trim the excess PVA tag off. With practice you will be able to attach fresh bags in seconds.

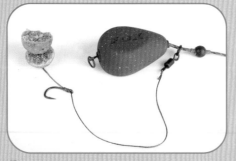

7. Because the weight of the PVA bag is concentrated under the lead the helicopter PVA bag rig can be cast long distances. When the Network micromesh dissolves the hook bait is presented right alongside the contents of the bag.

8. Before tying a fresh bag to the lead dry the lead off with a hand towel, removing any water trapped inside the lead insert. Bags can be tied in advance and stored with long tag ends ready to be knotted to the lead swivel.

SOLID BAGS WITH HELICOPTER RIGS

SOLID sheet style PVA bags can also be used with helicopters, the bag tied around the lead and the hook length left outside the bag.

After sprinkling enough pellets in to the bag to cover the bottom, allow the lead to sit at the base of the bag, filling around it with pellets. The bag can be compacted and tied off with tape as usual, gathered around the lead core or tubing above the lead. Over hard bottoms slide the stop bead and hook length swivel on the lead core down to just above the top of the finished bag. The hook can also be nicked into the bag for improved casting. Over soft bottoms the lead will no longer sink so readily into silt, the size, shape and density of the filled bag ensuring a much slower descent and softer touchdown.

"Solid sheet style PVA bags can also be used with helicopter rigs, the bag tied around the lead"

PVA STICKS

A REFINEMENT of PVA bag tactics, 'sticks' use combinations of powder and groundbait fillings to create tightly compressed PVA parcels of bait inside the mesh of continuous Network PVA.

By relying on finely milled down, chopped or powdered ingredients only to add attraction around a hook bait, when the PVA mesh around a stick dissolves it leaves a small area of highly attractive groundbait with the hook bait the only solid food item for the carp to find. It's a great way to boost the pull around a hook bait, especially in conditions where carp are unlikely to feed hard, for example through the winter.

The tactic revolves around using PVA friendly liquids to create the stick mix groundbait, so the filling doesn't dissolve the PVA mesh and it only breaks down after casting.

In the warmer months you can mix fish oils or hemp oil with your groundbait or stick mix until it is damp enough to compress. Through the winter concentrated PVA friendly bait dips and soaks are a better alternative, dispersing smell and taste more readily.

PVA sticks are mounted lengthways on a rig by drawing the hook length through the centre of the groundbait inside the mesh, concealing the hook and helping to hide the hook length.

Because the hook is safely tucked into the groundbait inside the PVA, a stick rig can be cast anywhere, even into weed without any fear that your hook will be masked.

It's another great go anywhere, catch a carp tactic for any type of venue - a perfect one mouthful trap to catch carp of all sizes.

STICK FISHING TIPS

- Almost any powder can be used to boost groundbait, whether marine pellet powder, corn steep liquor powder, green lipped mussel, chilli powder or commercial extracts such as squid.

- Sticks produce best with bottom baits. Short 8-12cm hook lengths and small hook baits like 10mm boilies, chops or plastic corn with size 9 and 10 LS Arma Points are perfect.

- Start with sticks around 5-8cm in warmer weather, keeping them consistent for casting accuracy. In colder water try tiny sticks of 2-5cm with high levels of powdered additives mixed with dips.

- Drop your stick rig in the margins and watch it dissolve. Is the groundbait obvious or does it blend in discreetly? Try darker stick mixes matched to the colour of the bottom on heavily fished venues.

- Avoid lead safety clip end tackles with PVA sticks. A safe, effective lead clip rig will jettison the lead every time you cast if a stick is attached to the hook length, bouncing the lead off as it hits the surface.

TYING PVA STICKS

1. First make the PVA friendly groundbait. Here we're adding Activ-8 dip to crushed hemp stick mix.

2. Damp the groundbait down with small splashes of dip and mix it up until it just squeezes together in your hands.

3. Fill the centre of your palm with mix and pour it down a narrow Network Micromesh funnel.

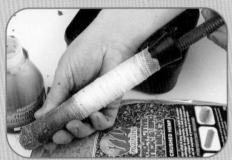

4. Gripping the PVA tight to the sides of the funnel compress the groundbait down into the tube using a PVA plunger.

5. With the plunger push the finished stick out the bottom of the funnel and tie it off tightly with an overhand knot.

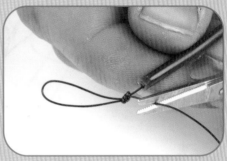

6. To allow PVA sticks to be loaded on to hook lengths finish your rigs with a figure of eight loop rather than tying a swivel on.

7. Fox Kwik Change swivels allow stick baited hook lengths to be replaced quickly and easily without retying hook lengths. Use them with in-line or running lead end tackles.

8. Slide a Kwik Change Sleeve on to your looped hook length using the stix needle, then bait the hair.

9. Thread finished PVA sticks up a stix baiting needle, ensuring the needle exits the side of the stick not the centre where the PVA knot is.

10. Locate the hook length loop into the latch key end of the needle and pull the hook length steadily back through the stick until the hook tucks into the side of the stick.

11. Locate the loop into the Kwik Change Swivel on your end tackle and push the Kwik Change Sleeve over it to secure it.

12. Here's the finished stick rig ready to cast. You can load rigs with PVA sticks in advance whilst fishing, allowing stick baited hook lengths to be replaced and recast within seconds.

PVA STRINGERS

BEFORE PVA bags were readily available PVA string was the only option for presenting free baits alongside a rig. PVA 'stringers' involve threading baits on to the string with a baiting needle. You can use any size baits and any number of baits but the bigger they are and the more you use the less well a stringer casts.

PVA string has improved dramatically, but always had disadvantages. There has always been a tendency for anglers to knot the stringer to the hook which delays dissolve time considerably. Because PVA string contracts as it dissolves there is also a danger that unless baits are generously spaced on the string the PVA string can fail to dissolve at all. Plenty of more experienced carpers will have had the misfortune to wind a PVA stringer back in still attached to the hook even after several hours in water - not ideal.

These days PVA tape has made string or mesh tape redundant. Very fine with a diameter of 10mm Fox Fade Away PVA tape dissolves readily, gone in seconds even in very cold water. Its width helps grip baits so they can be spaced to retain their position on the cast, and hook points can be simply pushed through the tape to attach a tape stringer to the rig without any danger of extended dissolve time.

Although widely overlooked in favour of bags these days PVA stringers are still a great tactic, grouping a number of larger baits like boilies, nuts or meat tight to the hook.

A couple of boilies or half baits on Fox Fade Away PVA tape with a hook bait of half boilies is a great tactic for pressurised carp wary of large baited areas.

Fade Away PVA tape is great for tying off the necks of solid sheet style PVA bags. Wrap it around and tie off with a simple granny knot.

Before casting a few turns of PVA tape around anti-eject rigs that use sliding rings and hairs along the hook shank prevents any possibility of tangles or the hair twisting.

A.
Accuracy ... 92.
Advanced Rigs ... 190,204.
Antiseptics ... 42,43.
Anti-tangle Tubing ... 48,103.
Armadillo ... 84,103.
Artificial Mixers ... 146.

B.
Bait Bands ... 145.
Bait Droppers ... 100.
Baiting Needle ... 182.
Birdlife ... 147,166.
Bars ... 18.
Blood Knot, Three Turn ... 64,65.
Boilies ... 208-213.
Braided Lines ... 72,73.
Bubbling ... 18.

C.
Carp Care ... 38.
Carp Senses ... 10,11.
Catapults ... 102.
CHILLCOTT, Ian (Chilly) ... 192,193.
Chod Rig ... 205.
Clipping Up ... 94,95.
Coloured Water ... 18.
Combi-rig ... 192,193.
Comfort (winter) ... 168.
Commercial Fisheries, Key Features ... 34,35.
Controller Floats, Types ... 144.
Controller Rig ... 145.
Cork ... 146.
Corn ... 163.
Cortex ... 192,193.
Crashing ... 18.
Creeping up to Canopies ... 98,99.

D.
Depth ... 21.
Dips ... 165.
Direction Markers ... 26, 94.
Distance Markers, semi-permanent ... 96,97.

E.
Elevator Lead ... 54.
Estate Lakes. Key Features ... 32,33.
Ezee Loader ... 234,235.

F.
Feature Finding ... 26.
Feeding Times ... 168.
Feeders ... 110,111.
Feeling Leads Down ... 20.
Feeling The Bottom ... 27.
Figure of Eight Knot ... 64,65.
Finger Stall ... 87.
Floater Fishing ... 138.
Floating Pellets ... 139.
Fluorocarbon ... 68,69.

G.
Gravel Pits, key features ... 30,31.
Grinner Knot ... 64,65.

H.
Hair Length ... 180,181.
Head and Shouldering ... 18.
Heli Kit ... 60,61.
Helicopterigs ... 60,61.
Hemp ... 163,219.
Hemp Pellets ... 163.
High Riser Foam ... 102.
Hooks (Arma Point) ... 172,173.
Horizon marker ... 24.

I.
Illusion Fluorocarbon ... 68.

K.
Kiting, Direction Dangers .... 130.
Knotless Knot .... 178,179.
Knuckle Rap .... 102.

L.
Lead Core Leaders .... 50,51.
Lead Core, Splicing .... 50,51.
Leads, in-line .... 52, 56,57.
Leads, Swivel .... 52.
Lenses, Polarising Glasses .... 16.
Line-Aligner .... 176,177.
Line Clip .... 131.
Loading a Method Feeder .... 108.
Location .... 14,15.
Locking Up .... 127.
Luncheon Meat .... 163.

M.
Maggots .... 163.
Maize .... 163.
Margins .... 18.
Marker Floats, Setting up .... 23.
Meat .... 163.
Mending the Line (floater fishing) .... 141.
Method Feeders, Types .... 110.
Method Groundbait, Mixing .... 112,113.
Micro Marker .... 24.
Monofilament .... 70,71.

P.
Palomar Knot .... 64,65.
Pigeon Mix .... 220.
Plumbing, When and Where .... 28,29.
Polarising Glasses .... 16.
Pop-ups .... 146,164.
PVA .... 230-243.

R.
Recasting .... 157.
Remote Sounders .... 169.
Rigidity Knot .... 64,65.
Running Leads .... 58,59.

S.
Safety Clips .... 62,63.
Scales .... 44,45.
Shock Leader Knot .... 84,85.
Skyline Markers .... 26.
Slack Line .... 122.
Snag Fishing .... 126.
Snag Rig .... 134,135.
Spod Capacities .... 86.
Spod Spill .... 87.
Spodding .... 80.
Spool Reducers .... 77.
Spooling up .... 74,77.
Stalking .... 118.
Stratos 12000 Mag .... 83.

T.
Tape Markers .... 94,95.
Tapered Leader .... 23.
The Method .... 106.
Threading Tubing .... 48,49.
Throwing Sticks .... 100,101.
Tippexing Hooks .... 146.

U.
Unhooking Mats .... 40,41.

V.
Variable Sensitivity (alarms) .... 167.

W.
Weather .... 160,161.
Weed Marker .... 24.
Weighing .... 44,45.
Wind Direction .... 18.
Winter Fishing .... 156,157.
Winter Location .... 158,159.
Wire Cutters .... 42,43.
Wrap Arounds .... 87.

Z.
Zig Rigs .... 148,149.
Zig Rigs, where .... 150,151.